FEATHERS IN MY HAIR

By

Renetta T. Womack Howard

DEDICATIONS

This work is dedicated to Crystal, Ember and Julius

INTRODUCTION

This is a new day and it is a scene which can escape you if you are not having much contact with the younger generations. It is possible to be completely out of the loop, especially if you are not into the latest technology. Believe it or not, many people still do not have a cellular telephone, a computer of any kind, or a flat screen television.

This true story is about a lady, my very best friend through the years, who was not completely out of the loop because she did own a desk top computer. She kept in touch with HER world with her computer. She had a cellular telephone, but its purpose was purely for talking and texting. At one time, she had even considered getting a Jitterbug, one of those telephones advertised for the elderly in the AARP Bulletin. It had large letters and numbers for those with problems seeing; a loud ring for those with problems hearing and it was easily portable.

This sixty plus year old lady, Janet J. Smith Myles, discovered additional amenities in the world of technology and found more feathers in her hair as she sought to find the love of her life after losing her loving husband with whom it had taken twenty-five years of sorry tears, disappointment and heartache in marriage and distrust of lovers to really connect with. Many names in this story have been changed to protect the innocent and the feathers in her hair.

THE FUNERAL

I was too nervous to really relax as my daughter drove to Boz, Texas from my home in a small town in Mississippi, Scroggy, where my maternal relatives had mostly lived and died. We were headed to Boz, Texas, the town in which my late husband, Randy Myles had been born and was going to be laid to rest in a couple of days. I had lost him to an ailment induced by his chosen career as a typewriter, copier, Dictaphone and VCR repairman. He had contracted Silicosis from the use of certain silicon containing cleaning fluids which he had used on the various machines.

As we rode along, I was thinking of the fact that when we discovered that he only had a short time to live, that we had purchased a house in Fort Worth, Texas and had put our Scroggy home up for sale. He had looked forward to moving to Fort Worth with me as most of our packing had been completed and the movers had been contacted and the moving date had been set. Murphy's Law would set in and he died the day we were supposed to move.

We had to get to Boz in order for me to finalize the funeral arrangements. My husband had bought a burial plot which he had paid for, but was still paying on the funeral specifications which he had been paying on for years and I still owed $1100. I also had to pay for the opening and closing of the grave, an additional $1200, which was not an option when he purchased the burial plans. I also had to choose a casket spray and have the funeral programs printed. My daughter had made them before we left Scroggy.

While we were at the funeral home taking care of business, we were shown my husband's casket and there were a number of beautiful flower baskets and plants there which had been sent by our friends and relatives. He looked so peaceful in the casket and had been dressed exactly as I had instructed. The registry showed the names of those whom had been to view the body and his children and their mother seemingly had been the first to see him. One son and his daughter had visited him a month before he died. That had been pleasing to him.

Once in the hotel, Randy's niece who lived in Boz came over and helped me to fold and staple the funeral programs and then we went to my sister-in-law's home who had arranged for a family get-together and would entertain the family repast after the funeral on tomorrow. The church provided a repast there as Randy had grown up in that church and participated in almost every aspect except preaching.

Most of Randy's nieces and nephews were present for his funeral. They had come long distances, some of them, telling me that he was their favorite uncle and it was no way that they could miss his homegoing. He was the youngest of thirteen children and there were only two left who were themselves very ill and unable to be there.

I was exhausted after the family gathering and quickly got to bed and to sleep the night before the funeral. The programs had been made and friends in the community accepted the various roles on the program. The only unknown person was the new female minister. The church at this time did not have a choir or a musician. A former pastor played the organ until everyone was seated.

The minister attempted to sing acappella and after a while, I could not take it any longer, so I got up and played *Amazing Grace* on the organ myself! I did not have any sheet music, but I had learned that song in the key of G Major.

I felt better after I sat down and individuals took the floor having their say about Mr. Myles. My granddaughter who felt that he belonged to her was more devastated than anyone. His own children were not as hard pressed as she was. I suppose that was because he had always been a fixture in her life from her birth up to this time, whereas he had not had the pleasure of raising his own children into adulthood. He had been a loving and helpful father, but never received the respect from his children which he had hoped for. He had supported them faithfully until they were adults, but their mother had kept him in a restrained position. He even tried to be as helpful as possible with his children's children but there were limitations. His gifts were often exchanged for money from the store of purchase. They could never tell him how much they enjoyed something he bought for them.

Just before we entered the church I was told that one of his daughter-in-laws was questioning my granddaughter about how our property and other belongings would be distributed after his death. She did not hesitate to tell her that she already owned the Cadillac car and my daughter advised that the house in which we lived did not belong to us but to my mother. That was kind of squashed.

After the repast in the church, I promptly distributed the flowers and plants to the family members who wanted them. The only plant that I had kept had been given to me in

Scroggy by the Preservation Commission and we had brought it to Fort Worth and left it in the house in which I was preparing to move into.

    We went to my sister-in-law Dorothy's and had the family repast there. We ate plenty and some members partook of some spirits. It was nice to have a gathering of familiar faces and people you called family. The next day, most of us would be traveling to our homes and having thoughts of happier days gone by. I certainly would. The years with Randy had been my most happy, loving and memorable years; years without feathers in my hair.

AFTER THOUGHTS

Randy and I had been married for thirty years. It had taken us twenty-five years to get married. We had decided in college, that we were to spend our lives together, but he was drafted into the armed service during the month of August, 1956, when we had planned to have our wedding. He decided to postpone it until later. I suggested once that he was in service, that we get married on his first furlough. He told me that his family wanted him to wait until his tour of duty was over. That would be normally two years. We had courted two years in college and I was a virgin. This could not be! He was in Los Angeles when drafted and I was in Chicago.

It would not be. David Smith had been my high school boyfriend and when he discovered that I was not getting married, he promptly began to call, come around and ask me out on dates with him. I had once been in love with him in high school and it was not difficult to be happy with and around him. I informed him that I was engaged still and really planned to get married to Randy. I did not mind seeing him but he had to know that. David became more obsessed with me and asked me to marry him. I put him off until Randy decided that he would go to see his sister in California on his first furlough instead of coming to see me and get married.

I had told him how my working and both of us saving would make it possible for us to purchase our first home when he was discharged from the army. I saw that my suggestion fell on deaf ears and decided to take charge. David was employed at the U.S. Post Office and had already served two years as a MP in the army. He and his mother had purchased a house together and he had recently purchased a new car.

He showed me his savings bank book and told me that he could make me happy. In addition to working, he was studying auto mechanics and body and fender repair on his GI Bill benefits.

I had my doubts until one Saturday morning, David called me and told me that he wanted me to go somewhere with him and he would pick me up. I got ready and went with him. He took me to the Sears Roebuck store straight to the jewelry counter. He spoke with the clerk who brought out a wedding set which he had chosen and asked her to make a fitting for me. I accepted the gesture and he paid for the rings. The clerk told him when they could be picked up. He bought the whole set, so I rather felt that he was sincere and agreed to marry him.

In the meantime, I wrote to Randy and told him of my plans. He voiced that he wanted to correspond with David. He did write a letter to him, to my address. I gave it to David. He let me read it. He told him that he loved me and if he did not really love me, not to marry me. David did not answer Randy's letter and that following June 8, 1957, we got married. I was now Mrs. Janet James Smith.

I already had my own apartment and David moved out of the house with his mother and into the apartment with me. My lease would be up at the end of February, 1958 and David felt that we should move into the house which he and his mother had purchased. I was not too comfortable with the idea, but his aunt who had lived in the upstairs apartment had moved out and into a housing project and his mother felt that we should move in. We did.

That was one of the sorriest mistakes I had ever made. Shortly after moving, I became pregnant with my first child upon the day that we had new furniture delivered as my apartment had been a furnished one. My mother-in-law was not happy when David told her about it. Her comment had been, "I thought ya'll had better sense than that by now." We had been married nine months at that time. I did not take too kindly to that statement and the irony of it all was that every job which I had applied for was now coming through but I could not accept it because I was pregnant. Employers did not want pregnant employees. They had to stop working before they started to show their baby bumps.

My aunt suggested that I should go back to college and take all of the courses which the school board wanted me to have in order to become a certified school teacher. I embarked upon that mission in the City College. I took a full load of whatever I needed. David was nice about letting me use his car, but so often it needed gas and he had not given me the money to buy it. Often, I graded papers for my aunt and she would pay me and my mother would send me money too during the month. That was how I made it, financially.

I would make a budget and give it to David in order to pay our monthly bills and no matter what figure I gave him, he did not give me a penny more. If I asked, he would turn his pockets inside out to show me that he had no more money. Crock!! As the recession during the Eisenhower administration deepened, I began to believe him, but in the meantime, I learned to inflate the budget so I could have some money without depending on my relatives. Once the baby was born, finances improved and David became more responsive. He mostly worked at night, so when he came in he was expecting breakfast before he went to bed. In order to have breakfast, he had to give the baby her first morning bottle of milk. It was an enjoyable experience for both of them. When I fed her, she acted really hungry and gulped the milk down. When he fed her, she would suck a while, smile and kick and look at him and them suck some more. I could not understand it, but my friends said that perhaps he was more relaxed in the process than I was. Perhaps they were right, because after breakfast, I had to prepare the formula for the rest of the day and bathe the baby and get everything cleaned up. David slept until the evening when he would get up and go to a part-time job at a restaurant. He worked there from 6:30 P.M. until 10:30 P.M. and then on to the post office. His hours there were from 11:00PM. until 7:00 A.M. He would get home in the morning about 7:30 A.M. to feed the baby.

    I secured a part-time job as a church secretary in order to purchase some clothes that would fit me because none of my 'before the baby 'clothes fit any more. I also wanted to get things for the baby. David swore that he could keep the baby while I worked the four hours. His mother was still working, so she was not home and the cousin who now lived in his old room was also working. The day that I came home and found that my baby had been crying enough to wet up the sheet; I decided that something had to be done. David had to quit the part-time job if he was going to care for the baby while I worked. We also needed to move, too, as his mother felt that it was her decision as to the kind of washing powder I was to use when using her washing machine. David had failed to get a washing machine for me because the day that I met him at the furniture store, it was raining and I did not have an umbrella, got wet and he was nowhere to be found. When he showed up, he had been looking at a pair of Floresheim shoes which concerned him more and I pitched a fit! He refused to buy the washing machine and I refused to wash. He had to do the washing in his mother's washing machine and I sent the baby's diapers to a diaper service. I washed her clothes in the bathtub and the kitchen sink.

The car was messing up and getting hot and one day I had to walk several blocks to get home because it stopped on me. David decided that perhaps we should get a new car as we did not want car trouble when we had the baby with us. David had quit the part-time job and with me working part-time, he felt that we could afford a new car, even though he did give his mother $60.00 per month on the rent. We paid our own utilities except water which was an address or building concern with the water department, not an apartment concern.

On the coldest night in the city, we went to have our new car delivered. We were trading the one we had, and that particular night, even though we got it started, we had a very hard time getting it out of the snow. A couple of neighbors helped us and we finally made it to the Ford showroom. We had ordered a white Ford 300 and when we got there, they told us that the only one available was pea green one and we liked it even better and accepted delivery. About a month after we purchased the car, I felt the need to move to an apartment away from David's mother, as she always saw David's side of any disagreement that he and I had. We did not visit each other and after the baby was born, he took her to his mother rather than have her visit us. I stopped being in her company after I finally told her how I felt; that I was an adult, not her daughter and she could not tell me what to do or not to do. If she thought she would bump into me as she came home from work, she would use the back door instead of the front door. She also did not know that David had shared with me the true ownership of the house. She wanted me to believe that it was hers alone. I never told her what I knew, but certainly gave her the idea that I did not give a care about what she said or felt.

She was sure of my feelings when I named our baby girl Mildred after her most hated sister-in-law. My mother-in-law could not stomach Mildred's presence. She felt that she did not treat her brother right. He would die and go to hell for Mildred and the more she tried to put a wedge between them, the closer he stood by her. I liked David's uncle. He was a very kind, gentle and loving man and enjoyed life with his wife. Mildred also enjoyed good friendship and camaraderie. She and I got along very well.

Tension did not improve and I decided that we would move; hell or high water I was getting out of there! Baby Mildred was about four months old when I found an apartment in Hyde Park and signed a lease to occupy the premises. David helped with the moving but was not very happy about it. After we had been in the apartment about three weeks, he was not happy and we argued and he decided to leave me and the baby. My part-time job did not pay enough for me to pay $80.00 a month for rent, eat and take care of a baby. He did not leave me any money when he left either. Fortunately, my mother had sent me a $50.00 money order which was just enough to get a train ticket to Scroggy. I got busy and my cousin Elwood's wife came over to help me get ready to go and would take me to the train station the next morning. I called my mother and she would meet us at the train station. She would keep Mildred for me until school was over in June. She and her sister shared a house and her sister was not working, so she would take care of Mildred during the day. I, on the other hand would return to Chicago and look for full time employment. I knew Mildred would be in good hands when I went back to Chicago the next day.

When I returned to the apartment, David had been in it and taken some linen and towels. I did not care. I went to the University of Chicago for employment as a secretary. They were ready to hire me, but the pay was only a few dollars more than what I was already earning part-time and after all of the various deductions, I would not have as much money.

I spoke to the church's pastor about my needing to find full time employment and leaving the part-time job. He asked if I would stay if my hours were increased to six a day, rather than four. I agreed because an additional two hours per day in a five day week would equal forty more hours of work and pay per month. I could budget and manage, except I now had to pay bus fare since David had the car.

I was scheming on how to make ends meet and David would call me and I would not talk to him. I was MAD! Some love this turned out to be! After a week of my hanging up on him, he came to the apartment and begged me to take him back; to just let him come back and I would never be sorry. He got down on his knees and pleaded and cried. I could not take the tears and finally gave in to him. I told him that I demanded respect and would not tolerate his foolishness.

When it was time for the next rental payment, David did not come home from work on time. When he did come, he was inebriated and in an argumentative mood and it turned into a lamp throwing spat. I did not hit him, but I broke the lamp. I had bought the pair of lamps shortly after Mildred's birth; the first thing I had bought on my first time out of the house after her birth. Fortunately for David, he had cashed his check and had given his money to a friend who was trustworthy. That friend did bring the money to us. David had however gone to sleep and was sleeping it off. I was shocked and surprised at his actions, but hoped that it was just a one-time thing.

When David woke in the evening, he was humble and felt guilty for his behavior and wanted to know what happened to the lamp.

Naturally, I told him. He apologized and I accepted his apology with the notation that nothing like that would ever happen again.

At night, our apartment was kind of creepy. It sounded like the people walking in the next apartment were really in our apartment. The gas refrigerator was really a freezer. It froze everything. I complained and by May, I consulted the real estate company for a nicer apartment. Spring break in Chicago was moving week. On May 1st, we moved around the corner to a three story courtyard building on Cottage Grove. We had a third floor apartment for the same amount of rent which we were paying in the first floor duplex. After careful examination, we figured that we were occupying the living room, smoking room, dining room and kitchen while the other side had the bedrooms; probably four. We now had a living room with a hide-a-bed, a dining room, kitchen and a bedroom. We had Mildred's baby bed in our bedroom.

We had not been in this apartment but a month when David came home again and he had been drinking alcohol. This was not like him. He had been sober and when we were in high school, he was one of the few boys who did not drink, smoke or use profanity. His friends used to tease him about his inability to curse, saying such words as "poot,' 'fart,' and 'do do' while they used more traditional profanity. He was rather quiet unless he really knew you and liked you, otherwise he never had much to say, but could talk incessantly if he knew you.

When I asked him about his condition, he went into a fury and actually struck me with his hand. I was no match for him, especially when I had not expected it, and when I had the chance I ran out of the apartment after I hit him with my shoe with all of the strength that I could muster. I did not know what shape he was in. I went and slept in the car. Later, in the morning before the sun came up, I looked up and there stood David trying to get into the car and recognized that I was in it. He told me that he had a terrible headache and did not realize that I was in the car. He suggested that I go into the apartment and sleep. I did get out of the car and went into the apartment. He later came in still complaining about his head, but got no answer from me. He did not seem to realize that I had hit him with a high heel shoe.

My mother had called and told me that she would be coming into Chicago with Mildred and that she planned to enroll at Roosevelt University for the summer session and start work on her master's degree. I was happy to hear it and happy to see my baby girl.

Our couch was what one called a dufold with storage underneath and it was more stylish than a futon. My mother would sleep on the dufold while spending the summer with me as we had not purchased a mattress for the in-a-door bed. When they arrived, I would have to get a baby-sitter for Mildred as my mother would be attending class during the day.

A baby sitter was recommended to me by one of my friends and I found her available to work. We had to pick her up and take her home. I would have bathed Mildred and fed her before I left for work. My babysitter brought a uniform with her in a bag and left with her bag when we took her home after work.

If I tried to call home during the time I was working, my phone line was always busy and when I got home, if my baby's diaper had been changed, I would find it in the bathroom beside the diaper pail, but never in it. Sometimes my baby had not been fed, but the sitter had eaten. Then, after about a few weeks, I noticed that I had sheets or pillow cases or towels missing. I had not inspected the sitter's bag each day when I took her home, but I decided that she was too expensive for me and the pastor of the church arranged it so I could take Mildred with me. I had a car bed. She was now seven months old and could sit up when she was not asleep and when the pastor was in, he would play with her. She enjoyed that.

I was happy for a change. Randy had called me. He was no longer in the army and wanted me to leave my husband and come to Boz with him. He had not gotten married and had not told his mother that I was married, but did tell her that I had a child. She talked to me and also asked me to come to Boz because Randy would take good care of me and the baby. She said that she thought that we should be together, as she knew that he truly loved me. I agreed to think about it because David was becoming someone that I did not know. I told my mother about it when she got here and her suggestion was to stay with my husband as I might be 'jumping out of the frying pan into the fire.'

The summer rolled along. My mother would cook dinner when she got in from school and when Mildred and I made it in, all I had to do was to feed us and wash and clean up the kitchen and dining room. David was working on a 3:00 P.M. to 11:00 P.M. shift now, so he would get home around 11:30 P.M. or close to 12:00 midnight, depending on the traffic.

I had completed my requirements to take the certifying test to become a certified public school teacher and made proper applications for the job. About the middle of August, I received a card notifying me that I was to report to Hirsch High School the day after Labor Day to teach History there. I told my pastor and he said that he was happy for me and he would find someone to fill the position when school started. His wife was a music teacher at the same high school where my aunt worked. I had told her first and she advised me to let her husband know in enough time to find someone to fill the job. I had complied.

Mildred was pulling up now and getting ready to try to walk. For the most part, she was a happy baby. She would seldom cry unless she was really sick. She would wake up every morning before I did and sit and play quietly with a toy in her bed. Once I started to move in bed as if I might be waking up, she would start to cough steadily and jump up and down in her bed. I certainly could not sleep with that. She was now drinking whole milk. I had burned up the sterilizer one day she was not feeling well and I was getting ready to take her to the doctor. In the rush, I ruined the sterilizer. I went out and bought another one, to be told by the doctor that she could now have whole cow milk and I no longer had to sterilize. The formulas had never really agreed with her digestive system, but I kept following the doctor's orders until she no longer needed formulas. That was a relief. He told me to give her more pork chops to chew on and some steak to increase her protein count.

In preparing for school, I found a friend who agreed to take care of my baby while I worked. She lived around the corner in the same building as two of my friends. I had met her through them. She had a son who was a month younger than my daughter and was happy to have a playmate for her son. Mildred had started to walk. David would take her to the sitter in the morning and I would pick her up in the evening. We always walked home and she had to stop and touch every flower or weed along the way. Steps were difficult for her, so when we made it home, I had to help her through that. It took almost an hour for us to travel one and one half block to our home.

I was surprised that David was taking Mildred to the sitter so early in the morning when he was not due to work until 3:00P.M. I found out when I cleaned his pockets to put some clothing in the cleaners. I found a check receipt wherein he had been paid for working in a bank restaurant. When I asked him about it, all he said was that he had taken the job a month ago. He did not want me to know that he was earning some extra money. It did not matter to me if he were happy as on my full time teacher salary, I was able to save some money and buy a bedroom suit and a mattress for the in-a door-bed. We had been sleeping in twin beds which had been bought as bunk beds because of the space in the upstairs apartment where we were when we bought them. We took the bunk beds to his mother's house and stored them there and used the new bedroom and slept much better.

We lived in the apartment for a year. My back porch neighbor asked me to get my clothes off her clothes line which covered the entire porch. I did and put lines in my kitchen and dining room as I washed diapers every day in the washing machine which I had used David's credit to obtain, in MY name. The Sears Roebuck salesman had been compassionate. David did not object and seemed pleased.

Our marriage seemed to be somewhat on track and we were not arguing, but still encountered some obstacles like our car being hit on the street by a drunk driver and David being robbed in the courtyard after stepping out of the car and losing his new overcoat and my cashed check which he was to deposit in the bank on Monday, before Christmas Eve, as Mildred and I had gone to Scroggy for Christmas. He said that he had called and told me what happened, but I was tired from the long trip and did not remember talking to him. My mother verified that he had called and she thought I talked to him. Sorry. I could not remember.

After Christmas when I returned home, I was a bit surprised to see David in another new coat. A small package came in the mail with his wallet in it and a note which said, "Found these papers by the "L" track." It contained David's IDs but no money. I had lost a paycheck minus the train fare and the money I kept to spend during the holidays. I soon got over it. I had left Mildred with my mother again as my babysitter had decided from my encouragement to return to school. She had studied beauty culture and dropped out after her son was born.

My sitter and I became very good friends and did a lot of things together socially. My other two friends began to complain that we spent more time doing fun things. One of my friends, Julie Woods, in that building had already begun to do and say some weird things and I had already started distancing myself from her. She would ask to borrow money or some clothing accessory and never returned said items. The last thing she borrowed were a pair of mants to wear to a dance. I told her that she could have them as I had bought her for the price of a pair of mants. I had used them when I got married.

It was not long after this incident that she took sick and pulled her children from the supposedly best public elementary school on the south side and sent them to her mother in Jackson, Mississippi. We knew something was wrong with her, but not sure what. Her husband, Darrin had hired a maid to keep house and take care of her. She appeared healthy, but spent a lot of time sitting outside the building and sometimes blocking the entrance in which my newest friend had to get into the building. This often led to confrontations between them because shortly after she sent her children away she would go to Myrle's apartment and play with our children until her husband's aunt told Myrle that Julie had contacted tuberculosis. Her husband, Darrin worked for the city water department and he was going to work every day. When I was working at the church, she would call there with messy stuff about me and Myrle and I had had it after one of the confrontations, she had Myrle arrested.

When I learned about it, I took Myrle to the police station to have Julie arrested. Myrle had not touched her, just demanded that she move so she could get into her apartment. Myrle refused to file the complaint telling me that "Two wrongs don't make a right." I told her OK and we went home. Myrle had to go to court and the judge put her under a peace bond. Myrle would not speak up for herself and that angered me.

Myrle was OK with the outcome. She did not have to pay a fine; just reside peacefully in the building.

Two weeks later, Myrle had her family over for a little celebration. They often came anyway because they loved to play bid whist and so did I and I was often there to join in the fun. They played cards, laughed, played music, imbibed a few spirits and enjoyed a fun time. I had not been there that night, but Julie called the police and told them that Myrle was breaking her peace bond. The police had found no disturbance and left after advising Julie that she did not thoroughly understand the peace bond. Myrle was not in any way breaking the peace with her, just enjoying family fun. After this incidence I decided that we should do something to make them think twice about meddling others and feeling that they could get away with it.

Myrle and I decided to call Julie's house and we spoke to the maid saying that it had been reported to the health department that was a case of tuberculosis in the home and we wanted to verify it. The maid answered, that, "Yes, Mrs. Woods has a touch of the TB." We thanked her and told her that the water department needed this information as Mr. Woods was said to be an employee of the water department. She apparently told Julie who in turn called her husband at work and advised him of the call. Later the next day, he called me and asked if I had called his house regarding Julie's health because he believed that I was the only person who would do that. I asked him if it were so and he had to admit it. I then warned him that if he did not control his wife's actions that I would notify his employer of his presence in the home and working with our city water as offensive. He assured me that he was not a contaminant. That, however, was the end of our friendship with the Woods. I had refused to take her daughter with measles to the doctor when I was pregnant and she was not happy about that, but I did not care at the time. My baby's health was tantamount to me.

When the year rolled around to May and moving day, I had again decided to move to a nicer neighborhood in Hyde Park and one with larger rooms and on a first floor as it seemed to take heat too long to get to the third floor. We moved to Kimbark in another court way building, except this time I had a back porch all by myself; no one to tell me to move my clothes off their line. In addition, the building had washers and dryers in the basement for a fee. I used the dryers sometime when it was too cold for the outside lines. Our new apartment had an in-a-door bed as well as the larger bedroom and Mildred's bed was still in our bedroom. I had bought the Danish Modern furniture and it was fairly large and demanded a large room in order to be comfortable. My aunt had moved to San Francisco and I shipped my cocktail and end tables to her and purchased some new ones from the store downtown which had sold out to Wieboldt's and they had bargains galore. I found a square Oriental black table with Formica top, and two black step tables with gold trim that I had to have. There were beautiful thick throw rugs of which I wanted two, lovely toss pillows, a long black entertainment table and a pole lamp that called my name.

I applied for credit to get the items which were selling at 50% of the retail price and took the form to David to sign so I get them and he refused to sign it. I had some money in the bank which I had saved and I paid cash for the items. They gave a distinguished air to our living room and David seemed to enjoy them more than I did. I reminded him of it 1too. He was happy to entertain company and felt self-worth. He was staying pretty sober, only drinking beer from time to time as he had not touched the hard stuff since he and my cousin dropped my washing machine from the second floor when we moved. I had to have a repairman out to fix it, as it fell on the controls on the top of the machine. Summer came and my mother and Mildred were back with us. I did not work during the summer and we did a lot of window shopping. Myrle and her son often went with us as I had a car and she did not drive. We went to the beach often and the ice cream parlors. The kids played in the park and I played tennis while Myrle watched the kids and crocheted. My mother was taking literature at Roosevelt and my aunt was attending DePaul University and they spent a lot of time talking about great authors: Thoreau's <u>Walden Pond</u> and a "Bee loud glade," and Shakespeare and his theatre. They enjoyed critiquing the works of great authors of literature and I listened and learned.

One day during the summer, I had left Mildred with a babysitter as I had some business to take care of and when I picked her up, she had suffered a fall and a knot on her forehead. My mother was furious and I suggested that it would get better. It was toward the end of the summer and classes were coming to an end. My mother packed up her belongings to go home and to her job and low and behold, she packed Mildred up too, and did not ask, but TOLD me that she was taking her home with her. I did not complain, but David was angry. He accused my mother of just taking his child. He soon got over it, I thought. This was an election year and he had thoughts on the political arena.

Just before the election, I was stretched out on the couch watching television when David called me from work and told me to come to get him. I had the car most of the time because he had the part time morning job and went on to the post office from there. I was working on the west side at an elementary school and I drove each day and picked up my cousin who also worked on the west side. Since I had not studied elementary education courses, she would brief me on how to teach the 49 first graders that I had in tacked down desks. Praise the Lord! One half had just come from kindergarten and the other half had completed a semester of first grade work .I wondered if David was sick because he did not usually call me to pick him up at any time before his shift was over. I got up and went to get him and there was confusion at the entry because he wanted to go back to his locker because he thought he had lost our savings book, but the guard would not let him go back. I could not understand it and he was really angry. We left, and on the way home he explained to me that he had been sent home because of loud talk about the election, and he was the only person singled out and after thinking about it, confronted the supervisor who had done it. The supervisor responded that he felt that he was being confrontational and should go home and cool down.

The next day, when he attempted to go back to work, he was given a suspension notice and arrested for assault on the supervisor. He had allegedly had a pistol that I had taken him and it was feared that he wanted to go back to the locker to do bodily harm to the supervisor. I called my pastor and he recommended a lawyer whom we both contacted as he posted bail at the jail nearest to the post office on 'skid row.' We got a change of venue and filed a complaint with the Civil Service Commission for a hearing. We were in court every other week and I was missing days from work going to court. I did not have sick days, so when I was not at work, I did not get paid. I was a full-time based substitute.

It looked more and more as if David would lose his job. At the Civil Service hearing, the supervisor's witnesses testified that David had a gun and threatened the supervisor. The workers who were to testify for David were not given the correct date of the hearing and he was terminated due to conduct unbecoming a postal worker. We still had to go to court to avoid a criminal conviction. That continued until the lawyer decided to have one witness at a time testify. On that particular date, all the witnesses were cloistered and call out one at a time and they all told the truth. The case was dismissed, but David did not have a job.

I decided that I needed a job which lasted the entire year because I would need to meet our obligations as David now only had a part-time job, though he was looking daily for full time work. His supervisor at the bank was a compassionate lady and when other employees went on vacation, she allowed David to work their shifts and she also gave him time to seek full time employment elsewhere. Her assistant was not so compassionate and when the supervisor moved to New York when her husband transferred, the assistant became the supervisor. David had gone to Skokie to see about a job and called me to call his boss to tell her that he would be a little late. She told me, "If he's not here by 10:30 A.M., he does not have a job!" I told him what she said and he did not try to go, he went straight to an employment agency and bought a job paying $50.00 per week. He had taken tests for state jobs and county jobs and was about to be hired as a city policeman, but I would not agree knowing his temperament, so that went out of the window.

After Christmas, I took a job as a County Caseworker in public assistance. I had to carry me, David and Mildred on my income tax form in order to get home with enough money to pay bills. It worked out fine. I was sending money to my aunt each month for Mildred's care as her daughter was with my mother. It was many years later that I learned that my mother did not know that I was sending money to care for Mildred because they had an agreement that my mother was caring for her school aged daughter in exchange.

We lived on Kimbark for two years and Mildred was now three years old and big enough to have a regular bed and her own bedroom, so I sought out a two bedroom apartment in Hyde Park with a moderate rental. I found a nice one that needed to be painted and took lease of it and painted it. I bought Mildred a full sized bed and painted the chest of drawers to match it. This was a second floor apartment. We had lived on a first floor and a third floor and now we were trying a second floor. That was the worst of all! The apartment manager lived beneath us, another "That's my clothes line owner" across the hall and furniture movers above us. Mildred liked having her own room. She could put all of her stuffed toys in the bed with her when she went to sleep.

During this time, I had taken a second job working at the post office downtown, the same one where David had worked, but on weekends. I did see his accuser supervisor and it shocked the hell out of him. Because I worked nights at the post office on weekends, David would take Mildred to his mother and she spent weekends with her and her new husband. Through the week, she was in bed by 8:00 P.M. The manager was always running up to our apartment if no more than to check on the painting. She did not want me to have my washing machine in the apartment and my neighbor across the hall had complained about me putting my clothes on her line on the back porch which took up the whole back porch. I strung my line right beside hers.

The neighbor across the hall from the manager was purchasing a home and soon moving out. The manager suggested that we move down to that apartment because she felt that my daughter made too much noise over her head and she could not get her proper rest. Naturally, I told her that it would cost just as much for me to move down stairs as it did for me to move upstairs and I refused to do that as I did not want to live on the first floor. She also said that some of the neighbors on the back end of the building felt that the child made too much noise. I did not explain to her that the child was in day care from 7:30 A.M. to 5:30 P.M. on weekdays and at her grandmother's on the weekend.

When school was out, my mother came to get Mildred and they went to San Francisco to be with my aunt who was supposed to have surgery which never took place, but they stayed the entire summer. In the meantime, I kept Myrle's son for her one Saturday and I did not try to keep him quiet. The manager came running up to my apartment about the noise. I told her, "THAT IS NOISE from this apartment!" She said that

I needed to move to the first floor. I told her that it was going to be easier for me to move out!

That night, Myrle and I went to a dance at the Trianon Ball Room and I had been looking at some newspaper advertisements of townhouses in Englewood costing only $12,000 with two bedrooms and a model was available for inspection. I could not enjoy the dance for wanting to see what it looked like. I convinced Myrle for us to leave and drive to the destination. It was dark, so the outside and the neighborhood was all we could see that night.

The next day, Sunday, I got my aunt to ride over with me to take a look at the model. She was not impressed but said that if I felt I could live in the townhouse which would be mine if I bought it, to suit myself.

David had been called from the eligibility list to work at the Chicago State Hospital in the supply department. That was way on the north side and he was doing part time work at a body and fender shop. I was still making more money than him. He had also begun to drink wine again and that was not easing my conscience. We had bought a smaller car and it was brand new; red flag for purchase of a home, but I went to the builder and made my case. He could not use me as the main wage earner because I was still of child bearing age. But, he told me to get the body and fender shop owner to give David a statement of his minimum wages per week, which added with his state job, would make us eligible for an FHA loan. He told me to tell the county credit bureau that I was not driving a car at this time. Sure enough, as soon as I got home, I got a call and I was sitting on the bed when he asked me, "What kind of car are you driving?" I could have passed a lie detector test when I told him, "I'm not driving any kind of car."

Our next step was to find the $500 needed for the down payment, $150 for a lawyer and another fee for the closing cost. We borrowed the $500 from David's mother who needed her money back soon though she had an employed husband, and then borrowed $600 from my mother to pay her back. By the time the deal closed, we had managed to have the other money we needed but were in debt to my mother for $600. We moved into our new home just after Thanksgiving. Mildred was so happy she ran up and down the stairs and even wrote

on the stairwell. We did not mind the running, but she had to wash the writing off the wall. She could not understand that as it was *our* house, not somebody else's. We had purchased a new stove and refrigerator at the courtesy of Sears Roebuck and I had portable clothes racks for cold weather and an umbrella style line outside for warm weather.

In the meantime, we bought a second used car for David to get to and from work. He left the body and fender part time job to work for Lien Chemical Company at O'Hare airport. On the weekends, he worked in the freight airport and Mildred and I would go with him and I made up beds for the pilots and cleaned the kitchen/break room. Mildred stayed with me and played while David cleaned floors and other items. I did some dusting and trash can emptying. My helping him gave us more time to get to a movie or do something that we wanted to do.

David was promoted to the printing department as manager, but was afraid to be in charge. I had to constantly urge him to be confident. He still did not feel confident and went to the Burlington Railroad seeking employment and was hired as a switchman. Again, he liked the job and the pay, but he was afraid to have responsibility. On that job, the man in the crew with the most seniority was the supervisor. David did not like this. He was a good worker, so it did not take long before he had to take on that responsibility. He increased his use of alcohol and it was becoming unnerving to me. Five years had gone by when I realized that he was an alcoholic.

In the meantime, Randy had been calling me and I had discouraged him. He was now a married man with four children. I asked him not to call me, but it did no good. David made some snide remarks sometimes when he knew he had called saying that I was more responsive to him after I had talked to Randy. I got angry behind one of his calls and decided to call his house. His wife answered the phone and said that he was not home. I told her OK and hung up. A few days later, his wife had gotten my telephone number off the telephone bill and she called me early in the morning. She said that she did not want me calling her house late at night because her baby was sick and the phone disturbed him. Angrily, I told her to tell Randy to stop calling me at night. Then she asked, "When did he call you?" I lied and said that it was a while back. She went on to tell me that she knew about me and his mother had told her about me and he has a picture of me that he keeps with him. I told her that I was not a threat to her and Randy; that I was married and a thousand miles away; that he was her husband, and she should make him get rid of the picture. She admitted that she had tried. I told her that I could not help her, the problem was all hers. I finally got her off my telephone and went to work. In a way, I kind of felt sorry for her.

I kind of felt sorry for myself too, as David's alcoholic stints were getting the best of me and my disposition because he became a mean violent person when he was drinking. I did not like fighting, but sometimes I had to, or run. It was not good for our child and we were both becoming enablers. That was the term I leaned when I sought help for my husband. On his 'off days' from work, he was drunk. I never knew what to expect when I got home any day. I guess a good stiff drink of something might have helped me, but I was not prone to alcohol. Something had to be done.

When summer arrived in 1966, I had decided that things had to change. I could not go on like this. My child did not need this and neither did anyone for that matter. I went to the public library and looked up the graduate schools with the least expensive costs and decided that I was going to move to my mother's, let her keep Mildred while I went to school.

When my mother arrived that summer, she was on her way to Washington D. C. to a Spanish Institute. She wanted to go to Mexico, but had not been selected for one there yet. We had paid her almost all of the $600 that we owed her. Before she left, I had not discussed my plans with her but David had been rude in one of his drunken stupors and locked her and the dog outside the house, telling her that he had paid her now and she could move on. She did go on to Washington and I got him to see a psychiatrist which seemingly made things worst. He took too many of the tranquilizers and Mildred screamed that I needed to call the doctor or her daddy would die. I sent her over to Myrle's who lived across the street and called the doctor who insisted that I keep him moving and try to get coffee into him. That was an all-night chore. When he was sober enough to understand me, I told him that I was leaving and I was making preparations every day to get away. I withdrew my pension from the board of education, hired a mover, filed for a divorce and started packing. I got my application in to a graduate school, but not all of my transcripts, just enough to get in and get away. I went to the doctor for entrance procedures to find that I needed iron every day.

SEPARATION

When I returned home from the doctor's office, David had cut his wrist and lay on the floor at the bottom of the stairs. I quickly left and went and got his uncle R.B. hoping to avoid what happened next. As soon as he got there, he called the police and took the dog outside, saying that he did not need to smell David's blood. The police came and locked me up in the paddy wagon with David, whose blood was shooting all over me and insisted that if I left he would do it again. The doctor at the hospital was ready to release him after he treated him to go home, but the policemen insisted that it was attempted suicide and he had to go to the county hospital psycho ward. Now Lord; that is a long ride in a paddy wagon with a man out of his mind and me locked in with him! I had to do it.

Once at the county psycho ward, David was again able to talk the doctor into releasing him. Here we were, on Chicago's far west side with no money and no car. I had enough coins to call home and I spoke to R.B. He told me to get a cab and he would pay for it when we arrived. All the way home, David threatened to hop out of the cab on the Dan Ryan Expressway if I left him. I did my best to placate him, knowing that I certainly could not endure much more of this. He was talking crazy and I had blood all over me. I needed a bath bad! We got settled and R.B went home and I packed more.

When the movers came the next day, every time they picked up something to put in the truck, if he said that he wanted it, I told them to drop it. I took our bedroom suit, the stove, the end tables and the pole lamp and one chair from the living room and the piano; the dining room table and china cabinet. I left everything else, and Mildred and I were on our way to Mississippi. My mother had made it back from Washington, but she had to take a course at Southern Mississippi University and asked me to stay until she returned. I did, and shortly afterwards, I was on my way to Atlanta University in Atlanta, Georgia with no idea of really doing anything but being away from David Smith. I did not believe in divorce and neither did my pastor, who had suggested a separation to think it over and then if it did not work, it would be the first time he had condoned a divorce, but David had cursed him. It had an impact!

I used my pension money to pay my tuition and room and board and gave the rest to my mother to be used for Mildred. All I wanted was some peace and quiet and away from the smell of wine and any other alcohol. I went to class and looked out of the window most of the time until my political science professor suggested that I needed to pay attention in class and put more effort into my work. He was also looking for a wife and I had been told that he had been asking questions about me and discovered that I was married. I told him when he asked. By Christmas, he had found a wife and gotten married and for some reason he seemed more at ease around me.

I found out that his wife was not really what he wanted and he was ready to throw in the towel. He tried getting closer to me and asked me to write an article in the *Harvard Journal* with him to rebate an article printed in it. I agreed to do it, but in my room, rather than some place with him. It was years later when I was sick that he wrote me a letter and told me how he really felt. By then, I had returned to David and was still married. It almost made me mad!

I had a roommate at AU who was just out of college. She was from Tougaloo, Mississippi. Her mother was a home economics professor at Tougaloo. She was attending school on a grant, and so were most of the students there. I learned that one other student besides me was paying cash for tuition and room and board. I had not had time or the intuition to apply for a grant or anything else. I was getting away from my alcoholic husband. When I learned of the availability of grants and scholarships, I applied for one and was told that I might be eligible for a work study program. It turned out that I had earned too much the previous year to even qualify for that, so I just let it be and concentrated on making it a worthwhile effort. Because my funds were short, I did very little socializing. I did not have funds to pay to have my papers typed and I did not have time to type any for anyone else, so I could not make any money. Therefore, I did not have money to use carelessly. Because I was married, I did not agree to be entertained by the available men on campus. I went out once with a gentleman in my French class who was more of a platonic friend than a suitor. We went to Paschal's Restaurant and Nightclub to hear Wes Montgomery, a jazz artist. There were two other times that I ventured out and one was to play bridge at a church benefit and the other was to go to Morehouse's Centennial anniversary. I probably would not have gone to that and from that day to this cannot remember the name of the gentlemen that my friend Mayme and I went with. Morehouse men were standing on the street asking ladies to go with them and we were snubbing them until our dean of women in the dormitory told us that they were Morehouse men and we would not be around for another centennial celebration. We went and enjoyed it, even though those gallons of alcohol on the table sort of made me uneasy. Frankly, I had never seen bottles of alcohol that large. They matched the appearance of the gigantic cake of Morehouse's first building which was about six feet wide and twelve feet long and about four feet tall. I understood that John Johnson of Johnson Publishing Company had a huge responsibility in its presence. All said and done, it was an affair that I shall never forget. It was worth my being vilified about a one of a kind book which I had refused to let the next user have while I was at the celebration. I had to return to my studies once back in the dormitory and

I knew that she was not the kind of person to give it back to me. Therefore, she had to wait until I was finished. There was a lot of flak, but I made it through the day of my presentation unscathed.

In the meantime, it was brought to my attention that my husband had moved someone into our home a couple of weeks after I was gone. He told me on the telephone that he had rented Mildred's bedroom to a young couple. I learned later that he had rented her room to a young man, but the female there was with him, David. I did not concern myself with it, as Randy had learned that I was in Atlanta and I believe my mother had given him the telephone number, because he called me and wrote me letters, begging me to marry him when my divorce was final. He told me that he was getting a divorce as well, but he had his children with him. He also sent me pictures of himself, but I was not ready at that point to make any kind of commitment to anyone. I had encountered a nightmare one day about David and his girlfriend in our home and together, they had beaten me and I was bleeding and woke up crying. I had taken a serious turn to my studies and getting back to my child. I had a lot of time to think and try to figure out what I had done wrong as to why I had so many feathers in my hair. I thought about my struggle to secure our family a home of our own. I thought about Mildred being our only child and the reason I struggled so hard. Had I walked off and abandoned all that I had worked for? My child deserved the fruits of my labor; not someone else or someone else's child, but mine. What should I do?

At Christmas time, I had planned to go to Chicago to my Aunt Verna's house. My mother and Mildred would also be there for Christmas. I did not plan to have any real socialization with David. All I wanted from him was my driver's license renewal and some money and/or credit cards so I could get Christmas presents for Mildred. I had left him with all of the credit cards and most were in my name even when his credit history was used to get the card.

The day after my arrival in Chicago, I called David to ask for my driver's license and the female there answered the telephone. I asked to speak to David and when he came to the telephone, I told him what I wanted. He claimed that he had misplaced the license and was looking for it. The female took the telephone from him and told me that she was not a roomer, but she was David's woman. I told her that I did not give a good concern, that all I wanted was my license and if she chose to be a whore and slut, that it was her problem, not mine. She told me that when I saw her that I would take back those words. I hung up.

About a half hour later, my aunt's doorbell rang. It was David. I answered the door and let him in. He gave me $25.00 and two credit cards. I told him that I did not appreciate his whore's attitude and decided that I needed the car as well. He was hesitant and I decided to look out of the window to see where he had parked and upon viewing, I saw a female sitting in the passenger seat. I felt strong enough to pull up one of those posts holding the chain around the grass and smashing the car and her with it. Instead, I hit David with a right hook that busted his eye lid and attempted to go downstairs to carry out my vicious intents. I tried to push him over the stairwell, but my aunt got between us as I attempted to get out and I found out how strong she was. I could not budge her. Once I calmed down, she cleaned David's eye and I became more determined than ever not to be disrespected. My lawyer had ignored my calls regarding my divorce and now I wanted revenge. He had called David after I left town and asked him if he wanted a divorce, according to David. He said that he told him "No" and he did not proceed with filing the proper papers though he had my money to do so. David said that he also told him that he could file on me for desertion.

Once my aunt cleaned David's eye, I told him that I wanted the slut out of my car and out of my house; that I was going to live in my house this Christmas. He cried and told me that he would get her out. I took the credit cards and gave him time to get her out. He came back later to get me and took me shopping for a housecoat, gown and female articles as I did not take a stitch of clothing with me except what I had on.

We went to one of our favorite restaurants and had dinner, and then we proceeded to our home. Upon arrival, I was in the kitchen and David went upstairs to be met by his woman coming down the stairs into the kitchen. I had a hammer in my hand and dialed the police, as I had no idea what was on her mind or what she intended to do, especially after I had been threatened earlier in the day. She had a bottle of gin in her purse and insisted that David leave with her. By the time that the police arrived, he was trying to get her to leave and she was insisting that he saw things her way. I told the policemen that I called and wanted her out of the house. She was tugging on David and wanted me to leave. I stood watching. The policeman finally said, "Which is it Champ?" He told the officer to take his "girlfriend." I signed the warrant papers and they took her on out and put her in a squad car and left.

David said to me that I did not have to do that. He was sorry that she was going to jail. I thought I had hit him earlier in the day, but when I struck him then, I knocked him into a chair and it slid all the way over to the picture window and the wall before coming to a stop. He had started to cry. I did not give a care! They had been sleeping on the floor on a mattress because he had not bought a mattress and spring for the bedroom suit he had purchased. The hide-a-bed mattress had a large hole in it where they had been smoking and drinking and set it afire. I put clean linen on the mattress and slept on it; not very good sleep.

The next day, my mother and Mildred would arrive in Chicago. Upon that arrival, it did not take me long to figure out that my mother and my aunt had definitely decided that Mildred would not be staying at home with me and David. It was well, because all we were doing was arguing and fighting. I did go shopping and bought Mildred some items for Christmas. I saw a few of my friends and we had Christmas dinner at my aunt's house. It was pleasant with a subtle skepticism and apprehension about our entire situation.

Once the holidays were over, David and I agreed that I would return to my home and he told me to take the keys with me. He advised that all would be well and he would call me regularly and perhaps drive down to Atlanta to see me. I pleasantly took all of that with a grain of salt. My mother and Mildred returned to Scroggy to complete the school year there as well. I was working very hard that second semester as I was now seriously planning to graduate and obtain the master's degree. Getting back with David was not really a high priority on my list but I did not tell him.

Things went well until one day David called screaming at me that his knee was swollen and the snow was so bad until the patio cover which I had installed had fallen and covered the entrance to the back door and knocked the light on the ground. I listened a while and told him to make the best of it as I was not coming to fix it and hung up. I had the feeling, that sixth sense that his woman friend had moved back in anyway. I had plenty of time to think and I had decided that he could keep her, but I was keeping the house for my child. I had decided that he and his woman could leave. I would make it and Mildred and I could be happy without him, his alcohol and mean ways. I did not give him any idea about my plans until a couple of weeks before school was out for the summer.

My majoring professor had recommended me to go to Tuskegee to teach stating that it was a beautiful place to raise a child and that I would be hired before I completed my degree as long as I kept working on my thesis. I made the application, a half-hearted one, and went on to Scroggy to get Mildred and return to Chicago. My professor felt that I should not go back to

Chicago and my husband, for my child's sake. I gathered that he had spoken with my other professor whom had been concerned about my marital status as he stated that I seemed to be trying to make the best out of a bad situation. Call it what you may, I returned and Tuskegee wrote and told me that I had not completed my application but they would keep me in their files and notify them when I completed my thesis. I agreed to do that.

About the middle of June, 1967, Mildred and I took the train to Chicago and got off at the 63rd Street station. We took a Taxi to our home. I expected to find only David there, or perhaps no one. No one was there but there were indications that someone had been there that day. I found some clean linen and straightened up the hide-a-bed; turned the mattress over on the un-burned side and put Mildred to sleep. About 2:00 A.M., David came in and neither of us seemed happy to see the other one. We had little to say. I was sleepy and he was tired, so we left it at that.

The next morning, I did as much as I could to clean up the house and make it half way decent to live in. David spouted about how I had left and took everything with me and had come back and did not bring a damned thing back with me but my funky ass. I told him that I did not plan to bring anything back and if it made him feel good, he could take what I <u>had left</u> there with him and his whore and move it to wherever he wanted.

He still had not purchased a mattress and spring for the bedroom suit he had bought, but he had purchased a stove. I had left the refrigerator and he had gotten our kitchen table set from his mother's house. There was no washing machine, so I used a commercial one until

I could purchase one. I went to Sears Roebuck where I had an account and bought some pots and pans and dishes and a coffee pot. After cleaning the kitchen very well, I purchased some food and cooked for us. I had to make certain that my child was fed properly. I also borrowed a hack saw from Merle's husband and took down the patio cover which had fallen and bought and installed a light at the back door. I did not ask David for help. One neighbor asked for posts from the cover and she put them in front of her garage. The rest of it was hauled off as trash. I had a clean topless patio which never would have fallen had David and our next door neighbor not had a fight before I had gone to Atlanta. He got so angry that he grabbed the post and shook it until it broke in the middle, still attached to the roof and floor. The heavy snow with no attempt to remove it, made it cave in. I cut my loss.

The next day, I went downtown to the Board of Education to apply for a teaching assignment and was told that I had to be out a complete calendar year and it would not be up until August. I did not change words. I marched right out on Wacker Drive and walked around to the Public Assistance Office to apply for a caseworker job. I was told that the last day to file an application had passed, so I asked if they had any other positions. I was then asked if I had any experience with the agency and replied that I had worked about four years as a caseworker. The clerk said, "Fill out this application, take it over to the county building and tell them to put a stamp on it and the test will be Saturday. We expect to have the results on Monday. Call this office and we will have the eligibility list posted." I did as instructed and prepared to take the civil service test that Saturday. On Monday, I called and was told that I was number two on the list and to come down and fill out my W-2 and other forms. I hopped to the decision. I was to report to work on July 5. I felt good.

On July 5, as I prepared to go to work, David took the distributor wire from the motor and generator of the car so I could not crank it and went to the park with it in his pocket. I called the police and stated my case. One of them went down the alley and raised the hood of a junk car parked near the train track and came back with a distributor wire and attacked it to the car. I thanked them and got to work on time. When I returned in the evening, I found the wire on top of the refrigerator. I did not say a word about it, neither did David. As usual, I fixed dinner; we ate and prepared for the night.

Mildred had located one of her Howalton Day School friends and she was on the telephone talking much of the day. She spent time with Myrle's son when David worked during the day, but he mostly worked at night, so she would stay home with him while I worked. I called as often as possible to check on them and she would call me to make reports. Unless she was at Myrle's house, she had to stay inside until I got home, with the doors locked. My key latch child; she was happy though. She loved her father and always had. She was his protector!

As soon as I made a paycheck, I went to Sears Roebuck again and ordered a full sized mattress and spring for Mildred's bed and one for David and me. I bought new linen and towels also. Now, I could get a good night's sleep, I felt. I also purchased slip covers for the hide-a-bed and the matching chairs in the living room. I had left the Hi-fi, so there were four pieces of furniture in the living room and a table lamp on the Hi-fi.

The next month, I purchased a washing machine and hung clothes outside to dry. I had fold-up racks to dry on for when the weather was bad. We seemed to be improving our relationship somewhat, but I still wanted a divorce. I called my lawyer and insisted that he file for the divorce as that is what I had paid him for. He went on and filed it. I did not tell David and when the summons was issued, the bailiff gave it to Mildred. Again, he said that he did not want a divorce. I listened and later told the lawyer that I was not going through with it. He was mad as hell! He told me that I needed to pay him for filing. I told him that he already had all that he would get from me. He said that he would write it off as a loss; I asked him if he called it a profit when he was supposed to do it and didn't. No answer.

Another Christmas came and Mildred wanted toys to play with the boys in the neighborhood as the girls were a bit older than she and were not interested in playing with her. She wanted an air rifle, a set of six shooters and a bicycle. I bought her a doll with hair that she could fix and a popcorn maker as well. She was happy and I realized that she could also play with her Daddy with those boy toys.

Mildred did not go back to Howalton Day school as I did not feel like waiting to see if someone would cancel, so she was enrolled for the first time in public school in our neighborhood. By Christmas, I was thoroughly disgusted with her progress. It seemed that she had been placed in a very slow class and I had asked the assistant principal about a change but was met with a lot of flak and no actions. At the time, I was being tested for cancer and was not at my best friendly person self. Mildred complained every day about feeling bad and I took her to the doctor who stated that she did have a fever and it could be a number of things. He gave me a prescription and I gave it to her. The very next day, I got a call from the school to find out why Mildred was not in school. I told them that I would be right up to the school. I left out the house looking crazy and mad! I met David who tried to get me to go back home and wait before I did something stupid. There was no talking to me about this.

I arrived at the school and told the assistant principal and whoever called me, that they were not concerned about her or they would have acted a long time ago on my requests to test her to put her in a proper class; to remove her from a class where the students could not read or talk properly as she came home and laughed about them. They amused her. She was not making any progress and I was not happy. Move her to a more suitable room or I would go downtown and complain. I showed them her prescription and told them that the placement for her was sickening.

Shortly after this incidence, I was hospitalized for a cone biopsy which turned into one hemorrhage behind another until I had to have a hysterectomy. I was in the hospital for six weeks and the day that I was discharged, I had another hemorrhage and had to return. My doctor thought that I would die that night. He gave me morphine and spent the night at the hospital on my account. He did not want to lose me. He did not realize that I did not plan to go then, nor the night in which I had emergency surgery and pints of blood. I had seen the light at the end of the tunnel! He had spent that night with me too. He and my aunt sat in my room and talked until daylight and he took her home.

During this time, hospital policies did not permit children in hospitals to see adults or babies for that matter. Mildred was worried about me as no one told her how I was doing. Whenever she was allowed to talk on the telephone, she always sounded as though she was going to cry if not already doing so. That bothered me too but I had to stay another two weeks until my doctor felt that the danger of any more bleeding had passed. He also advised me that I needed a divorce. He said that each time my husband visited me, that I had a setback afterwards. He said that I was afraid to let go and do better, but even though I might have my heart broken again, think of all the fun I would miss in between time.

I was discharged to my aunt's home and I was there a week when I discovered that David had spent $600 of the $1200 which I had saved and in a weak moment put his name on my account. I had hidden the bank book, but he had searched until he found it.

Another time at my aunt's house that I tried to push him over the stairwell. I decided instead to go home though I could barely walk upright. I had to maneuver the stairways backwards instead of forward. When I got home, I was ready to kill David. I called the police and they made him leave for the night.

I was miserable! My child seemed to have had a personality change. She was not her usual sweet self. She became selfish and demanding. I had worked only a couple of weeks in January and none in February and now it was almost Easter. I had to postpone the NTE (National Teacher's Examination) that I was supposed to take in February until July. I was not happy about that. I was totally dependent on David now, but I looked forward to better days. I grew stronger each day. I had to depend on Mildred to help me more. She was nine years old and could do a lot to help me. She was mostly cooperative, but when I told her that I could not get her an Easter outfit, she had a tantrum! I went to Wieboldt's and opened a credit account just to get her an Easter dress, hat, purse, shoes, socks and a light coat. She was happy; I tried to be.

By the end of March, co-workers called to tell me that my ex-desk mate who was working in the Intake Department had died and the job was open which would be good for me so I would not have to go out into the field to see clients. I called and asked for the job and it was given to me. I started working right away and none too soon. I wanted to be in good spirits to pass that teacher's examination in July. I worked in Intake until August as I had applied to teach again and had passed the elementary grade teacher's written examination. I would begin work in September at the same school I had left two years ago, with the same class. The oral examination was not scheduled until January, 1969.

During the summer, I had saved some more money and decided that it was time for us to move to a nicer neighborhood and buy a house built on its own foundation separate from the next door neighbor. We would have to put the townhouse up for sale if we got a federal loan we were told and that is what we wanted to do. I borrowed a couple of thousand dollars from my aunt to make the down payment and would pay her back when I resigned from the state job and drew down my pension. That was the plan and I followed through with it. David did finally go to the Veteran's Department and get the necessary paperwork and examinations to secure a VA loan. We had an FHA loan on the townhouse. We used the same lawyer whom we used when we bought the townhouse, only when time to close the deal arrived; we were shocked to find him not there for our closing, but one of his partners. He had moved downtown into a brand new skyscraper, out of the 'hood,' and was now big time. We closed the deal and got the keys and prepared to move into our Georgian home, the next day, a few days before Christmas. The house had a stove and refrigerator, much older vintage than ours, so we just switched. We took our later models with us and put the older ones in the townhouse.

About a month into our new home, reading the Sunday newspaper, I found the article about our lawyer being sent to prison for selling illegal bonds in the new office building. What a raw deal. He was the only Black partner in the firm and took the fall. Why he did not know is unbelievable. After that, I found bumper stickers for my car that read, "Do not hit me, my lawyer is in jail." I had it put on my rear license plate frame and still use it.

David was now earning over one thousand dollars every two weeks because of a lot of double shifts. He just could not stay sober. If he worked a week straight sober, he would be off a week drunk. It started to add up to me. I passed the oral examination and David's drinking seemed to increase. It was not long before he was suspended and dismissed from his job.

The townhouse had not sold and now I had two mortgages to pay. I decided to rent the townhouse especially after our real estate broker died and David was unemployed. Of course, he thought nothing of buying another job though he was looking for work at another railroad. He was told that the "Q" would hire him back after a few months off. He did not believe it and went to the steel mill and got hired there. That job did not last a pay period. One night, he just took off without a word and they thought he had fallen into molten lava. They called the house to ask me about him and I was able to tell them that he was home. But I did not say that he was being destructive. I had just put $100 down on a new Italian Provincial dining room set and it and been delivered just a few days ago and when he came in angry, he picked up one of the arm chairs, raised it in the air and threw it to the floor and broke a leg on it. I still owed about $600 on it and before I knew what I was doing, I hit him up beside his head with a punch that sent him staggering forcefully through the dining room door into the kitchen, splitting the door when it hit a cabinet and his rocky backward movement coming to a halt when he hit the outside wall of the kitchen. I was mad too! I was beginning to feel that I just might kill him, so the best thing for me to do would be to get a divorce. I had told my mother how I felt and she advised me that no one is worth killing; just get the divorce.

	I had a girlfriend whom had recently gotten a divorce and she recommended her lawyer. I contacted him during the summer as we were having a rough go of it. I did substitute work a couple of days and David had bought a minimum wage job which was some help. Naturally, I had saved some money to help tide us over the summer as Chicago schools during this time did not pay teachers the year round. You worked ten months and saved for the other two unless you knew you had a job or taught summer school. I felt that married teachers should not have to work during the summer. What's a husband for?

My new lawyer wanted his entire fee before he went to court. David was summonsed about the divorce and I asked him to move out. He swore that he was going to do right and even checked himself into the Alcoholic Treatment Center. After a few days, he had earned an outside pass. I went to see him and low and behold on the elevator with him, the smell of alcohol almost knocked me down and he wanted to rape me. I advised him that it would not work; he had to come clean. I was not playing this time. I left and a few days later, he was discharged. He went into the basement and slept all the evening, the night and into the next day. I believe it was tranquilizers. I calmly told him to find him a place to move and I would help him as his driver's license had long been revoked and I was paying for liability responsibility insurance on top of liability responsibility insurance because of his drinking and driving and trying to bribe policemen.

He found a room by the elevated train on 63rd Street and I helped him to move. He was there one week and Mildred and I went by to see him and anywhere you looked there was an army of cockroaches! I encouraged him to move back with his mother even though she was married now. There was a basement apartment where he should be able to live since his cousin was now in the apartment where we used to live. He was reluctant to ask his mother if he could move there, but I was not. I called her and asked her and she agreed with a lot of stipulations which meant nothing to me. Mildred and I took bug spray and sprayed everything that he had before we put it in the trunk of the car and again as we took it out. We got him settled in the basement which was a nicer addition which she added after we moved. It had a full bedroom. After I cleared David out, I got some more bug spray to make certain that I did not take any bugs home or keep any in the car. Mildred was not happy but felt better with her Dad at her grandmother's house. This meant that she could see him when she wanted to. She was very upset when I told her that we were getting a divorce. They often watched television in the basement on Saturday mornings and other times together and she did not want any changes. He was sleeping in the basement because I refused to sleep in the same bed with him or I would put three sheets on the bed making sure that we were not between the same two sheets. She told me that she did not see why he could not continue to stay in the basement as he was not bothering me. She did not want to live with either one of us; she was going to live with her grandmother in Mississippi! I did not argue with her, I let her exhale.

THE DIVORCE

In October, my lawyer had secured a hearing date for our divorce. He had had an earlier date, but because he had not been able to catch up with me to get all of his money, he postponed that date and got a later one. I secured two witnesses, one of my longtime friends who knew both of us in high school and my aunt. They could both testify to my trials and tribulations with David Smith. My lawyer promised me that I could get everything that I wanted. When the judge inquired of him as to why I should be awarded both houses that we owned, all he could say was " er rur,a, er rur," and the judge said that he could ask me and I told him that my husband and I had agreed that we would give the townhouse to our daughter and I would get the other house instead of alimony. The judge said, "So you and your husband agreed to this?" I said, "Yes, sir." He then said, "Well O.K., it shall be." He also awarded $100 per month child support for Mildred and put her education in my hands as well, until she reached her majority which was 21 years.

After we left court, we stopped downtown at Carson's and I bought myself a bottle of Madame Rochas Cologne. I had the need to feel liberated and to know that my twelve year fiasco of a marriage was really over. I went home and I cried and David came to the house and told me that he was coming back home, that I was still his wife. We both cried and he refused to leave. He spent the night and the next morning, I looked in his eyes and told him that it was really over. We were no longer married and he had to respect those boundaries.

While I was in court getting a divorce, David was being reinstated as a switchman by the Chicago Burlington Quincy Railroad Company often called the CB&Q, but simply the "Q" by employees.

They had merged with the Great Northern and were now the Burlington Great Northern Railway. I was very happy for David that he was back at work and would be able to fulfill his obligations as a parent, financially. It seemed that he and his mother and stepfather were getting along OK until the night that the astronauts were exploring the moon and his mother had gotten a call to come for David as he was sick. She asked her husband to take her to get him but he refused. Then, she called me, and at 1:30 A.M. in the morning, I got up, got Mildred dressed and coerced my aunt to ride with us to Cicero to get David. When I finally found the part of the yard where he was, he was in a tower. Friends of his had taken him there. He had been drinking and was about to make a mess and they told the office that he was sick and to call someone to come for him. I guess you could say that I was still an enabler.

I had been talking to Randy ever since I had filed for the divorce. The papers arrived the day before Mildred's 11th birthday. Randy promised that he would see me in the New Year, 1970. I had no idea that a divorce was like a death. It is the death of a marriage and mine had been very sick for a long time. Randy's calls helped me some but he was not there with me and I still felt alone and somewhat afraid. I had the complete care of a child in my hand and an even more frightening concern that David may not meet his obligations. I spent a good part of my day checking the positives and negatives and trying to map out a positive route for me to take. I checked out anything that I felt would help me to help myself. I started taking Human Relations classes. I was afraid to go out with a man. I felt like a helpless school girl. I had been out of the social loop too long. I had no idea what a date entailed. I did not know anyone whom I trusted so I was just out of it until my cousin's wife and her sister decided that I needed to get out and meet people. Her sister and her husband owned a tavern called the "New Journey's End," and took me out to it. I loved to dance but I did not know the current crazes though I was a quick study, and I did not drink alcohol. I decided to be sociable and try the Crème de Cocoa which I had poured into milk.

It became known that I drank 'milkshakes.' That drink did not make me act silly. I had tried a 'pea picker' once, lime juice and gin and I **did** act silly. I knew not to repeat that fiasco.

A social club held parties at the tavern on Sunday evenings. You could buy a voucher and there would be drawing wherein you could win a variety of items, the main one being a bag of groceries. The partying usually started on Thursday nights which was 'Lady's Night,' and it picked up momentum on Friday at the end of the work week and Saturday was 'disco night,' hot pants and all. The owner was a switchman for the Belt Line and many of his co-workers would stop in for a drink in the afternoon before work and then again after work around 11:30 P.M. It was on one of those occasions, close to Easter, that I met Shelby Williams.

Shelby had a reputation for being a lady's man. I was not very impressed with him, but he was fairly nice looking, tall, medium build and had a pleasant smile with the cute way he laughed. He had tender feet from the way he walked but he was a smooth dancer. He had a confidence about himself that I could not shake. He offered to make my child's Easter a happy one. I told him that her father would do that and he had just met me and I did not expect any such favor from him. He did not seem discouraged and became more enthusiastic when he discovered that his co-worker, with whom I danced most, had an interest in me. In the meantime, I inquired about Shelby and the only thing I could learn was that he did not seem to be married. He had told me that he and his wife were separated and she was in another state. I believed it when no one had ever seen him with a lady who was supposed to be his wife. I was still hesitant to give him my telephone number, but eventually did so. With Randy in the back of my mind, I did not expect too much from Shelby because I understood that he was a fun kind of guy and enjoyed partying to the hilt. I was torn between Shelby and my dance partner, and decided to date my dance partner. I made a big mistake. I allowed the fellow to visit me at my home and almost had to call the police to get him out. He came close to trying to rape me and my child was in the house. When I told her to call the police, he left. That was the end to that, dancing and all. I had cooled it with both of them and soon Randy would be coming to visit me. My hope hinged on that.

I had never owned a negligee and decided to buy one and have it when Randy came. My aunt had given me a beautiful black lace gown one Christmas about ten years ago and I still had not worn it because I told her that I was saving it to wear for a man who would really love me. That was as close to a negligee as I had come.

Randy flew into O'Hare and the flight was not really on schedule because the air controllers were on strike. I picked up my aunt and she and I took off to O'Hare to meet Randy. Murphy's law again, and when we got there, there was no sign of Randy. We looked and buses were also off schedule. After feeling that the trip was futile, I decided to go back home and a Caucasian lady asked if we could take her downtown as she was having a very difficult time getting a bus. My aunt told me to give her a ride. She would sit in the back with her and Mildred up front with me. Our return trip was fine until I got home and Randy called saying that he had paged me at the airport with no luck. I told him that we had done the same thing, with no luck. So, I got together and went back to the airport and again, 'feathers in my hair!' It had started to snow and on the bridge crossing some highways close to O'Hare; a driver hit my car in the rear. He was pulling a trailer and when he attempted to stop, the trailer kept pushing the car on the ice. We had to make a police report when our turn came, because this was not the only accident on the bridge. We finally made it to the airport and found Randy. It was some reunion. It had been 14 years since we had seen each other.

We got back to Chicago and we were too tired for me to show him my negligee. The next day was Easter Sunday. I cooked a nice Easter meal and my aunt took Mildred with her to an in-law Easter celebration. We talked to Randy's mother and his sisters on the telephone and they were still talking about me and Mildred moving to Boz. Randy's mother did not want him to leave Texas and I had already decided that Mildred would not attend a southern public school anymore. I did not tell Randy this at the time; I just went along with the program. He and Mildred got along fine, basically because he loved children and was a child spoiler. He took her to the store and bought her anything she wanted. This was right down her alley. She loved it!

Chicago encountered one of the worst blizzards that it had had in several years and especially in March. It had been warm and suddenly cold with foot deep snow. Because of this and the air controller strike, Randy had to get a flight back home, when he could, so he was there a few days longer than anticipated.

We vowed once again to get married to each other. We kept in touch writing to each other and talking on the telephone. Having been bitten before, I was not in a hurry to marry anyone because I could not bring myself to trust anyone. I had neighbors, co-workers and strangers who attempted to talk to me, but I was very slow to take the bait. From time to time, I would see Shelby and one day he told me that I should just go on, break down and let him take me out. Randy was in Texas and I was basically alone. I decided to go out with him and had a pretty nice time. He was off two days a week just like most switchmen. He never worked a double like David did, and unlike the "Q", he had to be near a telephone before each job starting time because he could be 'bumped' that day. The "Q" "bumped" for the next day. If you were signed up for a job today, it was yours but you could be "bumped" for tomorrow. He came to see me on one of his off days and we went to the race track or a movie or to a dance, or something fun each time. I was beginning to like Shelby.

One evening, I had a date with Shelby and I noticed now that he had a baby's car seat in the back seat of his car. He told me that he had a 2 year old that he took riding sometimes. For a minute, I bought that. He stopped at a tavern, left me in the car and went in to get a package of cigarettes. I thought to myself, if this man is married, I am in a very dangerous situation. Not knowing his wife or what she looked like, I felt like a sitting duck in this car. When he returned, I told him what I felt, including the fact that I believed him to be married, as a baby's car seat, stationary in the back seat of the car was an indication that the car lived where the baby lived. He then admitted that he had not told me the truth because he did not want to lose me. I told him to take me home because it was over. I did not play second fiddle to anyone. He was pretty upset and angry, but did take me home and I refused to talk any further. When I told my friends at the tavern about him being married, they were shocked, too. They said that he did not act like he was married and had lot of girlfriends.

About two weeks later, Shelby called me one day after work on one of his off days and asked me if I would please meet him in the neighborhood lounge, "The Living Room" which was around the corner from where I lived. I walked around there and he was sitting at the bar and I sat beside him and asked him what he wanted. He told me that he wanted me. I told him that I could not see how he could work that in, as I was single and he was married. He told me that he had not always been a good citizen; that he had owned a policy wheel and stole copper rather than join the work force. He had also used women to help him steal credit cards and the like, but had never met a lady like me and he wanted me in his life. He swore that he would give me money or buy me things every pay day and would never come to my house empty handed.

I listened to Shelby and I told him again, that' I did NOT play second fiddle to anyone and I did not fatten frogs for snakes.' If he chose to have my company, he had to act like he was not married. That meant being available _**whenever**_ I needed him, for whatever I needed him. In the meantime, I was still corresponding with Randy and he was sending me flowers, cologne and other items.

I worked during the summer teaching Reading and when summer school was over, I went to Providence, Rhode Island to take care of my mother's baby sister following surgery which was long overdue, after she was released from the hospital. My other aunt had gone ahead of me to keep her house in order while she was in the hospital. When I arrived, she went back to Chicago and waited for my mother to arrive with Mildred who had spent the summer with her in Scroggy.

While in Providence, I met a young man whose name was Richard. He was a friend of my aunt and his aunt worked at the same daycare facility as my aunt. Richard was a skycap and I went out with him several times to the Elks Club. His aunt loved to dance and so did I. We often had fun together.

The Elks were having their convention in Boston and I had a friend who lived in Cambridge, Massachusetts, who met me at the bus station in Boston where we had dinner and then took the train to Harvard Square in Cambridge where I spent the night with her. The next day, I met Richard in Boston at the Amory where they were having drill contests. We went to some after parties with some of his friends from Providence and finally got a bus in the wee hours back to Providence. I was tired and prepared to get back to Chicago as my mother had called while I was in Boston for me to come home. I packed up and prepared to fly back. Richard upgraded my coach seat to first class for my trip back to Chicago and promised that he would soon visit me when he got his vacation. He also had an uncle called Bill and an aunt called Tiny, just as I did, who lived in Chicago. He did as he promised; he called me regularly and reminded me so much of Randy.

Mildred liked Richard, too and he introduced her to eating pistachio nuts. I wondered how I had arrived at going from being married to having several men interested in my future. I was spending more time with Shelby on his off days, talking to Randy and Richard and found that the brother of my friend who lived a few doors down from me was also interested in me. I went to dinner and a movie with him once, but it was something about him that reminded me of David so much and he was also a postal worker. That was a relationship that was not meant to be.

School started again and Randy had been busy cleaning typewriters for the schools surrounding Boz and had not spent as much time on my behalf as earlier in the year. I was going out more socializing at the club and attending all kinds of formal dances, plays, ballets and the opera. My aunt said that I was 'flitting' all over town. I was enjoying myself and did not have marriage on my mind. I did not want a husband now. I was doing alright by myself. Shelby was there to escort me any place I needed to go and then went home to his wife. I did not have to cook, wash, iron or none of those things for him; just enjoy him. By the end of 1970, I heard less from Randy and Richard. Richard did come to visit around Thanksgiving and when I would not commit to marrying him, I heard very little from him afterwards.

At Christmas, my mother came to Chicago to have the holidays with us and we had a wonderful family time. My aunt from Providence came and some friends of theirs from Scroggy had the holiday dinner with us. Mildred was happy because she received a cassette player rather than the reel tape player that I had bought her. As I looked back over the year, 1970 had been some year! My New Year resolutions entailed having as much fun in 1971 as I had in 1970. One of my casework friends had gotten some of us together to form a Keno Club and we met once a month on a Sunday evening in each other's home during the year. It was also a Christmas savings club. We put our money in the treasurer and split it up at the last meeting before Christmas. I usually took Mildred with me and let her play a board too. She enjoyed doing that unless one of the girls had a baby for her to watch.

The year rolled on and I was taking Human Relations classes because I still had some unresolved issues that I felt that I needed to take care of, and in addition, these classes helped me to achieve my 36 hours above my master's degree to place in another pay scale lane. It was during this time that my mother suggested that I take classes to get a master's degree in educational administration as I had started working on an endorsement which would not be creditable in another state. She encouraged me to get the master's degree as she had hopes of my returning to Scroggy to run for school superintendent. I had no such hope, but went on anyway and got the M.A. degree, a course at a time, while I worked full time. I did decide that I preferred teaching in high school rather than elementary since Mildred would soon be completing 8th grade and going on to high school. I took the History examination and passed. I had already passed the methods part of the test when I was certified in elementary and no oral examination was required. Therefore, when I applied for a high school assignment for the fall of 1972, it was forthcoming. Mildred and I still had the same time schedule again. I had been in the elementary school for several years, so I had to get acclimated to the high school again. It was not difficult, except some of the young men tried to make passes at me. I was wearing my hair long and I suppose I looked younger than my years. It felt good though to realize that the world knew I was still here.

Close to the Christmas holidays, I had to have surgery on my left breast again. I had a cyst removed during the spring and had gone off the payroll, but my mother sent me some money to pay bills and Shelby helped me to stay afloat. I had just began to recover financially when I had to go to the hospital again for drastic surgery and would not be able to return to work until well into the New Year. My mother came for Christmas which was a great help. Family friends came and cooked dinner and we had a merry time. My mother stayed on a couple of weeks after Christmas to make sure that I did not try to return to work, especially since the teachers union was on strike. I went the last two days to the location of my school's non-strikers. I parked my car several blocks away as some vehicles had been damaged on the picket lines. Once the bargaining was over, classes resumed, but people who crossed the picket line were called names and often found items like shoe heels, feces and ugly pictures in their school mailboxes. I threatened to sue if it kept happening to me. I had been involved in a car accident for which I had a court action in play and a day after I threatened to sue, my lawyer called me and I did not get any more scab pictures or anything else untoward in my mailbox.

The New Year, 1973 was a good year also. Mildred had become a rabid fan of the roller skaters and had me involved in watching the contests on television with her every Sunday evening. When they came to town at the amphitheater, I had to take her to see them. It was fun when you had certain skaters that you favored. Being an only child, quite often I had to be her company on outings such as with the skaters and naturally when The Jackson Five came to Chicago at the Black Expo sponsored by Operation Push.

Mildred and I both were enjoying high school. Both our days ended before the elementary schools therefore we had time to shop or see friends after our busy days. Our year passed swiftly it seemed. I was still 'flitting' around town as my aunt called it, having a good time. I taught summer school again in the elementary school in order to pay for a steel garage door which was lighter than the wooden one which I had. After the breast surgeries, I did not need to lift that heavy wooden door which was even heavier after a rain. I had also pledged to become a member of a teacher's sorority and that had kept me busy as well as dug deeply into my finances. I did become a soror which added to my social activities.

Things went very well for the rest of the year until early in December. I discovered that I had another lump in my breast, the one on the right side, this time. My doctor got me to the hospital without giving me time to get my business in order, making it necessary for me to call Shelby's mother to get in touch with him to take me to the hospital. Reluctantly, she did call him and he came right away. I had to get him to contact my aunt to take care of Mildred and pay some bills for me. He was cooperative and did everything that I asked him to do. When I was released from the hospital, Shelby came over every day and cooked for me and Mildred. I was thankful and realized that having a man around is a good thing, but I still was not ready to make a commitment of marriage to anyone. Companionship was great, but not commitment. My health improved and I was able to enjoy the Christmas and New Year holidays with a minimum of pain. I was able to attend the sorority's annual Christmas dance.

COMPANIONSHIP

At New Year, a distant relative from Scroggy and her club had a grand New Year's party and Shelby attended with me. It was at this party that I told him that for 1974, he had to make a choice between me and his wife as I realized now that I needed a man with whom I could depend on daily rather than having relays in a time of need. I had not heard much from Randy in 1973, so he was on my back burner. Shelby asked me if I really meant what I was saying and I assured him that I was serious. I had heard from some of my friends that he was no longer seeing an excessive number of ladies, just me, so I felt fairly certain that he would make a decision. I gave him two weeks to decide what he would do.

About a week and a half later, Shelby called me and told me that he was ready to move in with me. I made room for him and advised Mildred of the impending setup. She did not really like Shelby as well as she did Randy and Richard but she could tolerate him as long as he did not try to act like he was her father. She enjoyed going to the racetrack with us and playing cards sometimes and that was about the scope of their relationship. He did not spend a lot of time at home anyway. He usually slept late, got up, dressed and went to the tavern to play cards with the guys there before he went to work. Most of the fellows at the tavern were coworkers on the railroad. They worked and played together. He usually worked from 3:00 P.M. until 11:00 P.M. When the shift was over, he and his friends usually headed to a tavern and had a few drinks before going home. The taverns closed at 2:00A.M., and that would often be the time that he got home. That meant that I would usually be asleep when he got in and he would be asleep when I left in the morning to go to work.

Once Shelby moved in with me, I curtailed my social life which included other men   and remained faithful to him. We enjoyed family events and for the most part got along very well until late in 1977, when his wife sued him for child support and alimony. I had no problem accepting his having to pay her as I felt that all men should take care of their children. I was not receiving any support from David as his child support stopped when he left Chicago and Mildred was now in her second year in college in DeKalb, Illinois.

During this time, my college was having an all school reunion and I had been talking to Randy, and he wanted us to meet for the reunion. I agreed. He had given me his work number and he had written to me. We were going to meet for homecoming. It had been seven years since we had seen each other. I booked my flight to Texas and rented a car from the airport to get to the campus. Upon arrival, no one had seen Randy. I looked and looked and he never showed up. The festivities lasted for several days and no word from Randy, and believe me; everyone was asking me about him. The only thing that I could say was that he was supposed to come. Why he had not shown up was beyond me. When I returned home, I called him and all he could say was that he could not make it. I took it in stride and moved on.

Shelby told me shortly after I returned from the reunion that he would have to give me $50.00 less per pay period in order to meet his obligations as a father and husband. I agreed to this arrangement though I was not happy about it. As I thought about it, I said to myself that I had no part and no fun in getting that child into this world, why must I have to sacrifice? After a couple of months, I told Shelby that I was having a difficult time with my child in college and no help with that, that he would have to restore the $100 per month that I was missing. Christmas came and New Year and he had not replaced the $100.

One early morning in February, when I dressed to go to work, on Shelby's payday, I told him that this would be the day that I expected to see the correct amount of money due me or he would have to go. He was not aware that I had packed most of his belongings the night before except those on hangers. True to form, it was an 'off day' for him and when he came home that evening with the same sad amount of money, I took his packed items to the door and told him to put them in his car. The ride was over. He looked at me and laughed. I assured him that I was not joking and put all of his belongings by the door. Snow was two feet high and we had not cleared it from the front porch, so he had to traipse around the side of the house with his belongings to get to his car. I got my house keys from him and told him to change his address.

One of the big factors in my actions had come because Shelby and his aunt had sold the place of business which his father had owned in Jackson, Mississippi and he had gone to the Kentucky Derby with that money and had not invited me, but brought me a plastic key chain with my first name initial on it from a Stuckey's in Kentucky. He had also objected to Mildred's desire to cook a dinner for her dad while he was in town visiting his mother and wanted us to go out so they could be alone. He did not want him in the house. I reminded him that the mortgage was in David's name. He retorted that he had paid enough notes for it to be in his name. In addition, I suspected that the red head down the street had gone to the Derby with him, as she seemingly only got home a few minutes before him and had been missing at the same time. I had been observing both of them. It was time for a change. I also felt that since Shelby's wife was suing for child support and alimony that one of them may soon want a divorce and I was not planning to marry him, though Mildred had once asked me why I was 'bumping around' with him if I was not going to get married. I just told her that it was not in my plan.

In the meantime, I was a member of the Millionaire's Club of Chicago and they had a trip to Las Vegas planned during our spring break.

I had made reservations to take that trip though I did not have a traveling partner. I discovered that the hotel fee was double occupancy and started to cancel until the airfare alone outside the club would have been more than the club's airfare and hotel, so I kept my reservation and paid the occupancy price for the room. I kept my belongings on one bed as a lounge and I slept on the other one. No one could believe that I went to Las Vegas alone, but I did and had a great time. I 'washed that man out of my hair!"

When I got back home from Las Vegas, I called Randy's mother's house and I spoke to his sister, who advised me that he had gone to Austin to an in-service meeting on some office machine. She also told me that he had left his wife. I said 'wife?' He did not tell me that he was married. She said that he had told her that he was going to call me when he got back to Boz and she was glad that I had called. As usual, I talked to his mother too and she was saying how she wanted to see me. No wonder Randy had not shown up for the reunion and did not tell me that he was married. I was in a semi-shock. However, when he did return to Boz, he called me and explained what had transpired when I would not move to Boz. He had been in a 'shacking' relationship with the lady he married when he had visited me in 1970. After I flatly refused to move to Boz, he went on later that year and they got married, but he felt that he had had his fill and it just would not work, so he was getting a divorce and if I still loved him, we could get married. He wanted me to come to Boz and see if I wanted to live there and if I did not, he would move to Chicago. That was difficult for me to believe, but it showed another dimension to our relationship. I was game.

When I severed my ties with Shelby, I also changed my furniture. I bought a white French provincial bedroom, living room and dining room furniture and gave my mother the Italian provincial living and dining room furniture and stored the bedroom for Mildred since her father had bought it. I later gave Shelby her old bed as she now had a white French canopy bed. He had bought the king size bed that I had, so I gave him a bed when he got an apartment. I was now ready for new adventures.

NEW ADVENTURES

Randy and I talked on the telephone, made cassettes and sent them to each other and wrote at least every other day. Our telephone bills made history. By July, I had decided to go to Boz. Randy met me at the airport and was a roomer with a friend of his. He got a room for me at a hotel downtown. I was there for July 4th and he carried me around to meet his family and some of his friends. He took me out to several eating establishments for dinner and showed me some of the highlights of his town. It was a pleasant trip. I was happy and Randy seemed to be happy as well. Saying goodbye was sad because we had not seen each other in eight years.

At the end of August and for Labor Day, Randy came to Chicago to visit me and we had finally committed to each other and we went ring shopping. He made a down payment on a wedding set that I liked and had it sized for me and I bought the matching ring for him. They would be ready before my birthday. I would be traveling to Boz for my birthday.

I was fairly content in this relationship until I received a disturbing telephone call from a young lady in Boz who told me that she and Randy were getting married. He had promised her and her children that they would be married. She had found out that he borrowed money from her to take me out when I was down there. He was practically living with her she said. I was shocked and hurt. It appears that there are always feathers in my hair! I was also angry. I called Randy, who claimed that he had been fraternizing with the young lady, but it was over and she did not want it to be over. He sent me the rest of the money to pay for the rings and pick them up to take with me when I went to Boz in October. After some crying on my part and some lying on his part, I decided to go through with the trip. Braniff Airlines was seeing a profit with our monthly flights. My October trip to Boz was fulfilling. We officially became engaged to get married. At Thanksgiving, Randy was in Chicago and Christmas I was in Boz. At the end of January, Randy's divorce had been filed and would be final in February. We made plans to get married in March. I chose March 24th as it was double the date of his birthday which was on the 12th so he would never forget our anniversary.

March came in 1979 and Randy and I were married at the Jackson Street Christian Church in Chicago. We were both members of the African Methodist Episcopal Church, but a classmate of mine from college was the pastor of that church and we decided to have him officiate our wedding. My mother and my aunt from Scroggy came to Chicago for the wedding and close family and friends were present at the nuptials in which my mother stated that we had to stay together because the minister prayed us together. She had never heard so many prayers at a wedding. They apparently had cement because we were married for thirty years. My friend Myrle hosted our wedding reception.

When the school year ended in June, I had put my house up for sale and packed up to move to Boz, Texas. During the spring break, I had gone to Boz and we had found a house that we bought and Randy had cut the grass and cleaned up everything before I was ready to move. He came to Chicago to help me to drive to Boz after the furniture was loaded for moving. We took our time and spent the night in St. Louis, Missouri on our way to Texas. We arrived before the furniture, so we spent the night at the Motel 6. The furniture arrived the next day. It did not take long for us to get settled in. I had a few days to get my business settled and get back to Chicago as my daughter was graduating from college and I was a candidate for a master's degree in that same ceremony. I also had to check on the sale of my house as I was hoping to close the deal at that point, but the buyer had obtained a mortgage from the city using bond money and it would be possibly September before the deal would be closed.

    The graduation ceremony was grand and our family celebrated with a dinner at a fabulous restaurant afterwards. I had planned to return to Boz until school opened as I planned to work a semester and take a leave for the rest of the year. Mildred already had a job which was a continuation of her internship in Psychology and was living with our aunt. My mother went back home after the ceremony and before I could depart, we got a disturbing telephone call that our family home had burned. I went to Scroggy rather than Boz. After two weeks in Scroggy, I took my mother home with me. Mildred had planned to go to California to connect with one of her high school boyfriends. I had taken her bedroom furniture with me and told her that she could have it shipped to California when she decided to go.

    Unfortunately, Mildred's job ended because the hospital closed the section in which she was employed and then she decided that maybe she could go to Boz. Upon arrival, I took her to job interviews and was seeking employment myself, but we were both sent to the same places, so I let her interview because I knew that if I interviewed she would not get the job as I was more qualified with experience for each offering. I had planned to return to my job in Chicago anyway, so it did not make sense for me to apply. I did return to Chicago after Labor Day and to my job at the high school. Randy worried me to quit and come home. I managed to get a doctor to sign leave papers for me to leave before the semester was over and I worked about six weeks on the new school year.

    The Pope was coming to Chicago and I was leaving. Catholics were lined up all along the Kennedy Expressway to wave at the Pope and the bus on which I rode to the airport had to go through the military section to be admitted to the airport terminal. There was a shut down until the Pope was out of the airport. I barely got my plane to Texas.

I was on leave from the Chicago public schools and decided to be a substitute in the Boz system. The substitute pay was $27.00 per day. I was earning $125 per day in Chicago as a certified teacher. I substituted pretty much when I chose to. One snowy day I was called and refused to go, so they did not call me for a couple of weeks after that.

Around the last of April, I received a notice that a job was opened with the Human Resource Department and I was eligible to be hired at $1200 per month. This would be steady work with some benefits, so I decided to try for it. I got the job and it worked well for several years. I was surprised to find one other Black person in the department and she had sued to get her job. When I applied for a higher position, I was denied it and I sued. I did not get the job, but I got pay compensation for discrimination. That did not sit well with the powers that be, so they gave me hell until I finally resigned, after a suspension, for using profanity where a client is supposed to have heard me and which I dared them to fire me. I was not fired, but a month after the situation; I resigned and took off to Chicago before I had a nervous breakdown. I had left my husband, mother and daughter at home. Randy helped me to drive back to Chicago, to find that had I been back a month earlier, I could have claimed my old job. I was not discouraged; I could be a substitute and just enjoy Chicago without thinking about the misery that I had encountered in Boz as well as the low pay for jobs and depression.

Randy had agreed for me to take this time and see if I could re-establish myself where I could feel validated. He wanted me to be happy and told me that if I could feel happy in Chicago again and wanted to make it my home, that he was willing to make the move to Chicago. My mother had long stated that though some of her worst days had been spent in Chicago, she was willing to sell all of her property and move there as well. She wished me luck.

My aunt was happy to have me living with her and my Uncle Bill. He had always been one of my favorite people, from my childhood and even when I lived with them before my first marriage. He liked to see people happy and would do whatever he could to make it happen.

It was cold in Chicago as we well know; snow and below zero temperatures sometimes. To make certain that my twelve year old car could withstand the climate, we had it rechecked and bought a steering wheel wraparound lock for burglar protection. We had learned from an earlier experience that the brake to steering wheel lock was no good, as that was what we had on the Cadillac that was stolen when we had come to Chicago for a family reunion in 1981. We had to get a bus back to Boz as we did not have enough money for both of us to take an airplane back there.

The bus trip was long and difficult. The driver from Chicago to St. Louis was sleepy and I talked to him to keep him awake until we made it to St. Louis safely. We had a long layover before we were to board a bus to Dallas /Fort Worth. Upon arrival there, we had to get a bus to Boz. Randy called one of his nephews to pick us up at the bus station and take him to his job where he could get a car to take us home. That was some trip. This time, Randy would take an airplane back to Boz as I would have the car we came to Chicago in, and he had his car at home in Boz as well as the new Cadillac which I had purchased that year that the other one had been stolen. After a week, Randy went back home. I settled in to be a substitute.

There was such a terrible snowstorm until it took me a half day to dig my car out of the snow. Once done, I did not want to drive it because someone else would take my parking space which was a bonus in a block where everyone lived in an apartment building. Therefore, I walked to the nearest bus stop and took the bus wherever I needed to go. Then, I did not have to be concerned about a parking space once I arrived at my destination.

I took several substitution jobs in elementary schools. Old friends at schools where I had previously worked asked for me when they found out that I was in the city. It was good connecting with them again, but time and things, after five years away, had changed. They were still the same, but the children were something different. I knew that I could not cope with all of the homemade African names; the Kieshas, Leshas, Jachori, LaDarrick, *etc.* If you did not pronounce the names the way they wanted you to, it became 'show time' in the classroom. The elementary students felt that substitutes were not intelligent and could not tell them anything. And, if you told them something that they did not like, it was time for you to meet their parents. Teachers were now hired by Neighborhood Counsels which was made up of neighborhood parents. Most non-tenured teachers were not happy about that situation, as it appeared that too often parents visited and berated teachers, even got them fired when they felt like it. This was not the Chicago school system which I knew and loved.

The teacher hiring system had been an aspect of the Chicago Central Board of Education. Teachers passed a written examination and if successful, were given an oral examination by a committee made up of principals and central office administrators. Now, some teachers were given certification after a number of years of successful teaching and my aunt referred to those certifications as Gift Certificates. There were a number of 'gift certificates' in the system now, as well as overzealous parents anxious to wield their educational power.

My aunt's landlord had the building furnace set to only give heat during the day and it would go off about 11:30 P.M. and come back on about 5:00 A.M. the next morning. I froze trying to sleep at night and suffered the 'Flu' because of it, I felt. If that was not bad enough, it turned warm early in March and the snow melted. Soon, water was dripping into my aunt's apartment and we had to try to cover everything up. The roof had holes in it and the 3rd floor apartment was taking in a lot of water and that which they could not get up was coming down into my aunt's apartment. The landlord was in the hospital and his ex-wife, the mother of his children and her husband came over and tried to regulate the furnace and made arrangements for the roof to be repaired.

In the meantime, I tried to get my aunt and uncle to move to another apartment, but they decided to stay where they were. I decided to go back to Boz. I had been in Chicago about two months and I had enjoyed some candlelight plays, a symphony and a couple of parties while I had been there. I felt a lot better.

I had also received word that my husband's ex-wife had been inquiring about my whereabouts and if I planned to return to Boz. I rather thought she would have suspected that since my mother and my daughter were in the home with Randy that my whereabouts should not have crossed her mind. Some of us just do not think like the rest of us. She had gone to my sister-in-laws to inquire about me. I wonder if she thought that I was leaving some kind of opening for her to return to Randy's life. I wonder. Was this the essence of that old saying, "You don't miss your water until the well goes dry?" Somehow, she never realized that her presence did not intimidate me, though I have been told that she did bear a resemblance to me; even my own mother agreed. Thoughtfully and thankfully, I put her and her plans and thoughts out of my mind and prepared to return to Boz with a positive attitude. I had a wonderful husband, a beautiful daughter, a loving mother, a nice residence and no bills. My husband could support me on his income and I was free to choose what my next step would be.

SCHOOL

When I first arrived in Boz, I was a substitute teacher. When I told them about my full time engagement, stating that I had taken a job, I was told, "You have a job!" I foolishly said, "This is volunteer work.' At the time when I had decided to return to school to get whatever Boz thought I needed to teach elementary school, the Board of Education was reluctant to give me information about the credits that I had or those that I needed. For all practical purchases, it appeared that my file folder had been put in the DEAD BEND. It took a while, but they finally came up with some information which I needed to enroll in the nearby college.

I had to take a couple of college level classes and a graduate class to fulfill the need for elementary science, mathematics and reading in the Boz school system as the certificate was for grades one through eight. My Chicago certificate was for Kindergarten through third grade. I did not want an intermediate certificate, grades four through eight. In Boz, Kindergarten was a different certificate.

I attended school several days a week and was now a babysitter for my oldest grandchild, a little sweet girl. Mildred had gotten married again and now had a child. My mother and I shared babysitting chores while Mildred worked. Her husband was in Chicago installing telephone systems in the new state building which was being built there. He was employed by GTE and often had to travel to other states to work. It was fun for me and Randy just loved spoiling the baby. She became his favorite person in a couple of months. My mind went back to the days when Mildred was a baby. Recollections flowed.

I established a routine of classes in the mornings and childcare in the afternoons. Then, I studied at night. Some afternoons I indulged in church and community activities.

I was very active in the church and the local NAACP. One day when I went to the local Black newspaper to place an advertisement for a community project, one of the owners asked me if I would mind coming in a few days a week and do some typesetting for them. I told him that it would have to be in the afternoon on school days, but I could come on a morning when I did not have class. It was set. This was a minimum wage job at which I leaned very much about the newspaper industry. I was learning and earning. I had no regrets. When I looked at the printed project, I had a real sense of accomplishment. I had a hand in it!

After completion of my college courses, I received the certificate for grades one through eight and a permanent certificate for administration. I had received a temporary one through reciprocity from Illinois. The administrator certificate had been my only state certificate. The one for high school social studies and Kindergarten through third grade had been Chicago certificates for life which were no longer valid since the Chicago schools were now under state guidelines. The teachers who had the city life certificates who were still employed were grandfathered in with the state and did not have to requalify. When I had planned to return to Chicago, I had taken the state examination to get the state certificate. I did not bother with the KGP certificate. Since I had graduated from a Texas college, I had a Texas social studies certificate for life. I was fully qualified now to teach in Texas and Illinois. I planned to explore my opportunities.

I planned to apply for a teaching position in the Boz school district. I had already taken the teacher-feared TCAT test and passed it. The employed teachers had to take the test and many of them failed and had to stop teaching. Some of the favorite employees who did not pass the test were able to keep on working when the head administrator approved the move. It was a hush- hush affair. They were able to keep their jobs until they retired. It seemed that there is corruption in many school systems.

    I applied for the job to teach in the Boz school district and could not get a response to my application except an interview, but no job. This was the year that Boz had to elect school board members by district rather than at large. The district had elected a Black female with whom the local NAACP President had asked to look into the reason I was not hired as a teacher. She obliged and was told that there was something negative in my file. She called me and asked if she could have permission to look in my file. I was happy for her to do so. When she called me later, she said that she could not find anything negative and that the Personnel Department would be contacting me soon.

    That same day, I received a call from school personnel that I would be interviewed by a couple of principals to see if they would hire me. I was sent to the Posey School and school was in session for teachers, but the students would not come until the next week. The Principal, Mr. Taylor interviewed me and said that he would hire me but his staff was full. I thanked him and went home. I had not been home an hour when the personnel officer called me and told me to report to the Posey School the next day to work.

    As instructed, I reported to the Posey School and was welcomed by the staff. I realized that I was in Texas and all of the bulletin and poster boards were huge. Most teachers had just about finished with their room decorations and I had to get started. I had to go out and buy materials to construct bulletins boards and get them up before Labor Day. I had to work on Saturday to get that done, and I did it.

    On Tuesday morning when the students arrived, I was standing pleasantly at the fourth grade room door to greet them. The students came into the room, mostly White, because they were bussed from a more affluent neighborhood, but their parents, upon seeing me, went straight to the office to see the principal and find out why the lady whom they had met was not greeting their children. I do not know exactly what he told them or why, but I learned that I had a room mother who would take care of class holiday parties *etc,* and I also learned that the parents would be in my classroom every week to see what I was doing. On one occasion, several parents met with me and questioned me about my educational background and how I taught various studies. I explained to them, that my qualifications were at the board of education and they could feel free to check it out; that I had been interviewed by the board and the principal.

Every week, there were complaints by some parents and every week there were praises by some parents. I took it in stride and looked forward to my monthly paycheck. I had reached my maximum pay in Chicago on Lane Three, a master's degree and 36 hours above the master's degree with fifteen years of experience, but I was being paid here for twelve certified years of experience with a master's degree. I was able to live on it, but it fit in to the old saying, "When you move, you lose." It was however, on par with the local economy.

I also learned that the sending school, the Honey School had a tutoring session for the students who were bussed to my class to insure that none of them failed. One parent came to me one morning with her son's paper explaining to me that he knew the answers and should have gotten a better grade. I explained to her that I gave credit for the right answers on the paper, not what he knew. She explained to me about the hard time **they** had getting the material correct. She went to the principal with it and even called the assistant superintendent, who in turn, called the principal. I was very happy when the school year ended and asked the principal for a primary grade for the coming year and he agreed to do so.

Just as I was preparing to get the third grade room ready for fall, the principal asked me, "Don't you have high school accreditations?" I told him that I did. He said, "I have a boy coming back here next year in sixth grade who was a terror, but I believe you can handle him. The sixth grade teacher is transferring and I need someone who can handle an older kid." Did I have a choice? No, but I wanted to work. Intermediate grades had not been my thing, but I knew that if I had to, that I could do it. I had had some challenges in Chicago which I had handled very well and I felt that Boz was not going to be any different now.

Posey was a CIMA school where all students were taught using accelerated teaching methods. As a result of working in such a school, I had to take CIMA classes during the summer to be called a CIMA teacher. CIMA meant *Curriculum Instructions for Maximum Achievements*. I also had to prepare for a different grade level, now, so I concentrated on sixth grade. Aside from the CIMA classes, my summer was quite relaxing and enjoyable. I went to a Church Missionary Conference in Atlanta, Georgia and to Chicago for a vacation. Randy went to New Jersey to learn how to operate and repair a new Royal copier and typewriter. Together, we had a 'staycation," that is a vacation at home. There were things to do in Boz that were fun, like Bingo and American Legion dances. We enjoyed those together and we participated in our church activities together. I sang in the choir, was Women's Missionary Society President and sometimes I was the musician for various occasions. Randy was a Holy Steward, a Class Leader and he sang in the Men's Chorus. We kept busy and had fun together. We also enjoyed time at home, watching television and listening to music that we liked. Sometimes, we even danced to the music.

That fall, I was ready for my new sixth grade. They had been bussed to the Honey School during the past year for fifth grade, and now they had returned to their home school for sixth grade.

I met them at the door and once they were comfortably situated, I made my seating arrangements and the young man who had been labeled the 'terror', had a seat right by my desk. He tried to intimidate me, but soon learned that it was a lost cause. Getting him in tow made it easy to control the rest of the class. He did get a couple of suspensions per school rules, but I was able to get his mother involved and that made a great difference. I established rapport with her and everything worked out just fine. We were able to keep him on track and the Sixth Grade Graduation at the end of the year was a beautiful occasion. It had been a wonderful year and I looked forward to the next year with pleasure.

The next school year, I taught the sixth grade, but the class that went to Honey for the fifth grade was the same class which I had taught in fourth grade and I would have some of those students in sixth grade this year. Because these students knew me, we were able to publish a school newspaper and sponsor and coordinate a Black History Month program.

The newspaper was free to the students, but we charged for advertisements and many of the students wrote personals which they eagerly looked forward to when the printed edition was available. We used the advertisement money to help to defray the publishing cost. The Principal's Fund paid the remaining amount. The parents were great supporters of this project and bought many of our advertisements.

We invited Black people from the community who were contributors to the culture of the city and county to speak to our student body during our weekly Black History programs. Each program included student and guest participation. This was something new to the Boz School and the community. The principal was proud about our programs and so was I. Only one thing brought an unhappy ending; our principal decided to retire at the end of the school year. We had a great retirement celebration but were very sorry to see him go. I personally had enjoyed working with him and had learned a lot about the Boz Independent School District.

I learned that when my principal retired that there would be an opening for a principal and an assistant principal and that I should apply for the assistant principal job. I did apply for the assistant principal position and was denied the position. I later learned that someone with less qualifications than I was given the job. I wrote a letter to the superintendent and my answer was that the person hired had more longevity in the Boz school system than I had and that is why that person got the job. I had a certified certificate in administration but the person hired had to attend school to get a certificate. That person was the offspring of a principal and was a favorite for the position. Nepotism and favoritism were at play. I was a transplant and not on the favorite list; qualified or not, I was lucky to have a job!

That fall, we got a new principal at Posey and I entered the school year with an open mind and readily participated in all of the administrative activities. Our assistant principal, who had been in that position the year before, and who had been a very pleasant person to work with under our Black principal seemed now to change colors as we now had a White principal and he was now aware that I was as qualified as he to do *his* job. I was slow to catch on until evaluation time. He had given me a glowing evaluation under the Black principal, but now, with the White principal, he reversed his stance. He told me that he really liked me as a person, but did not feel that I was doing the job as he thought it should be done. I advised him that he was entitled to his opinion no matter what it was or if I disagreed with him.

My class had continued to do the newspaper and sponsor and coordinate the Black History Month Programs. My students' test scores were up to par and my teacher evaluation was rock bottom. I sent my evaluation to the union representative after I was eliminated from the merit pay list and it seemed that I would lose my job. I was angry enough to kill the principal and the assistant principal as I knew and felt that this whole thing was a farce. It seemed that my applying for the administrative position put me in a bad light with administrators in my school, and especially the ones whose complexions were different from mine. As I left work on the day in which I was given my final evaluation, I opened the trunk of my car and got up in the trunk and took the tire tool out and prepared to go into the school and rectify the injustice which had been done to me. I could see blood! When I realized anything, I felt someone else in the trunk with me, wrestling the tire tool from me. I recognized my friend and the school secretary. She said, "No, no, Janet! You don't want to do that! Get out of this trunk and go home." Another teacher was leaving and inquired if help was needed. My friend Earnestine told her , "No, everything is OK." I calmed myself and got into my vehicle and drove home. I was almost home when I realized that Earnestine had followed me all the way home and into my driveway as I drove into the garage. I thanked her for keeping me from doing something which I probably would regret the rest of my life. I had felt that these two White men had decided that they did not need to feel a threat with me around and sought to eliminate it.

    The next morning, as I arrived at work, the principal advised me that he had made a mistake on scoring my evaluation and apologized for what he had done. I accepted his apology and proceeded to my classroom as calmly as I could. I did not want my class to know what was in my heart or had been in my heart. I had to make some changes. Any calmness which I now felt was because Randy always had a way of telling me that it would be alright. He said that if I did not have a job teaching school, we would still be alright. He always made any problem which I experienced feel like nothing more than a bump in the road; no big deal.

At the end of that school year, I decided to apply for a transfer to a school with a Black principal; a classmate of Randy's whom I had known in college for a semester or so. As a matter of fact, he was the only person in Boz whom I knew before moving there other than Randy. My transfer went through and I was welcomed at the new school and I worked hard to get my room set up and to welcome my students. I was to teach a third grade this year.

I soon learned that my 'friend' and principal was a 'chipper.' He was chipping with one of the young White single teachers. It appeared that they had gone on a South American vacation together during the summer. It came out in bits and pieces. After two weeks of school, this young lady was transferred to another school and I was transferred to the slow first grade class that she had been teaching. When the principal called me in about the change, he stated that he had to let somebody go, so he transferred her as "The buck stops here." I had nothing to say. I just accepted my position and begun work on it. He, the principal, assigned a young assistant to help me to get the room ready and I learned from her that he was dating her mother. I had to regroup. I thought, just when you think you know somebody that is when you need to not take anything you think you know for granted. I soon learned that the best demeanor to have is one in which you release as little as possible about yourself, knowing that word travels among the people who may or may not be your friends.

True to my feelings, the White female assistant principal was not happy about one of her favorite teachers being transferred and me, the new teacher, being put in her place. As expected, she did not like my methods of teaching either and came into my classroom to show me how to teach reading. I sat and watched her, gave her full range and when she left, I told her that I did not like her methods either. I also explained to her that there is no one way to teach anything which is the *right way*. I told her that freedom of methods was an option and she had no right to attempt to deny it to me. Naturally, my disagreements with her showed up on my evaluation. I appealed her evaluation and the superintendent sent someone from the central office to evaluate me. He did an acceptable job. I had been absent and was told by the principal that the assistant principal had told the superintendent that she felt threatened by me. It was during the superintendent's visit during my absence that it was decided to send someone from the central office to evaluate me.

After two years with my 'friend,' he and the assistant principal left us. He retired and she was assigned to be principal at another school. Our school received a new principal, a young man with whom I had attended an administrative workshop the previous year. He was happy to have me on board as he wanted me to sponsor the school's newspaper, but his White female counterpart, the new assistant principal, did not see me the same way. She was a carbon copy of her predecessor. She did not like me and did not mince her words about it. I was able to keep my job because the principal's evaluation offset hers.

One year as principal in this school and the new principal was transferred to a junior high school for the next year and allowed to take with him the teachers on staff that he chose to accompany him. I was included in that number and he assigned me some administrative duties which soon ended because a teacher had to be transferred and naturally, I had to take a full teaching load of five classes instead of three. I was fine with this. I did my job.

I was also appointed to publish a school paper for this school as well. Some of the language teachers were disappointed because they felt that their department should have been doing this since I was a social studies and reading teacher; not a language teacher. I just went along and did my job. I was happy. Randy was happy, so things were sometimes going our way.

Life was good except for the times when I had to have carpal tunnel surgery and then gall bladder surgery. Randy was always by my side and supporting and nourishing me. It was what I needed to survive in Boz.

TOGETHERNESS

I started to bowl in a league and soon Randy joined me. We were bowling every Thursday night. Randy had never bowled before, but it did not take long for him to rack up a decent average. We now had another activity which we could do together. We were both active members of the local National Association for the Advancement of Colored People and we were members of the same church and its various organizations and worked together there. Randy was an avid alumni of his high school and he participated in the school reunion preparations and I helped with that as well. When my high school and our college had homecomings, we went to those together as well.

As an officer in the local NAACP, we entertained guest speakers in our home following our annual Freedom Fund Banquets. The local president, Rose and I usually spent nights before the banquet putting the annual souvenir book together for publication and making tickets for the affair. Randy would make coffee for us on these occasions. He enjoyed being the supporter of these endeavors. He was just as helpful when we had an area missionary meeting at the church and we had to barbeque meat for the occasion. He was an honorary missionary and wore his white suit on missionary Sunday and sat with us ladies. I adored him. This was the kind of togetherness and mutual adoration I had longed for. I thanked God for this place in my life.

At the outset of this marriage, Randy's mother had really been the only person who was overjoyed about our union. This had been her hope from our days in college. She told me this. It appeared to me that my sister-in- laws were only concerned about how much Randy would gain, materially, by marrying me that would make their lives better. I gained this idea from one of my visits to Boz before we got married.

Randy and I had gone to his mother's house on our way to church and when we arrived, one of the sisters were happy to see us as there was something which she wanted Randy to do. She said that she had called her brother James, but he was ..."too busy being smothered in funk to come to see what we wanted." I could not forget what I had heard.

On another occasion, I had a fairly rude awakening when Randy's mother died. She had been fairly sick and in the hospital ever since I had returned from Chicago. We visited her in the hospital at least every other night and when at home, we visited daily. When she died, the family members gathered at her house where the two sisters lived with her. They would all go into a room and talk and map out the various arrangements. Randy would take me with him, but I was not a part of the discussions. On one occasion, one of my sister-in-laws told me that I was not a part of the meetings because 'blood is thicker than water.' I agreed, and really did not want to be a part of the planning. Money was involved and at that point, I was not feeling it. I later told my mother what my sister-in-law had told me and she quipped, "If she tells you that again, tell her that shit is thicker than both of them." I laughed, but it was a thought.

It was near Christmas when the funeral was held and naturally that put a damper on the holiday and that was our first Christmas as a married couple. My mother was living with us and Mildred had moved into her own apartment, but spent Christmas with us along with her fiancé. This was also the first Christmas that my mother did not have a home which she called her own. She very much missed her mink cape which burned and her wrist watch. Surprisingly, I had been able to purchase an excellent fur cape like the one she had and a nice wrist watch for her Christmas present. She was most overjoyed. The fun of the holiday was not the usual kind our family experienced, but in the wake of Randy's mother's death, it was not the kind of joy I would like to have. We survived and went on into the New Year with some kind of spirit. We had the music that we loved and received the presents that we wanted but the love just did not permeate the air in a beautiful way because of the grief. It seemed that we grieved a whole year and the next year, too.

The third year, I decided that I was going to enjoy Christmas like I always did and told my sister-in-laws that I did not plan to grieve another Christmas. I don't know what they told Randy, but when he arrived home from work that night, he was angry with me and hit me.

That was the final straw. I had told him before we got married that I was through fighting and it would not be a characteristic of my marriage and that I was packing and going to Mississippi where my mother was. I had purchased a brand new Cadillac and was regretting it, because I still owed on it and leaving would mean that I would not be able to continue to make payments, but I did not care. I was not staying in Boz and be mistreated by anyone. Mildred wanted to know what she was going to do if I left. I told her that she had a job, she could fend for herself. I moved into another bedroom to be away from Randy and prepared to move.

I do not know if Randy talked with his sisters or realized that I told him the truth about my feelings for Christmas or if he realized that he had made a dreadful mistake. He came into the room where I was sleeping and asked me to please listen to him. I sat up and told him to proceed. After I said that, he got down on his knees and asked me to forgive him and he promised me that he would never again, as long as he lived put his hand on me in any kind of negative way. He begged me to forgive him and let him love me like a man should and promised me that I would always be first in his life. He said that if I reconsidered and stayed with him, that I would never regret it. He stated how much he regretted what he had done under the influence of liquor and believing everything that his sisters said. He also promised me that he would stop drinking alcohol and always have a level head about himself. He hoped that I would not mind him having a drink on special occasions, but that would be the only time that he would drink. If he was not having a good day, he definitely would not turn to drink. He had already reduced his nicotine habit; no cigarettes, just the pipe now.

I loved Randy and did not want another failed marriage. I did not want to give up my lifestyle, but if I must, I must. I told him that I would think about it. I needed to sleep on it. My mother had bought another house in Scroggy and I knew she would be happy to have me there with her. I could find work there but I hated the thought of moving again. This was to be it! We had said that we would live separated in the house if we could not get along, but I did not want that. I wanted to be away if we could not get along. Mildred did not want me to go either. I slept on the thought and the next day I went to work and told Randy that I would stay. He was as happy as a lark when I went back to our bedroom to sleep. He made more promises to me and sealed it with a gift and a kiss. He gave me a necklace which he had a jeweler friend make. It was an open flower of yellow gold with a diamond in the center.

True to his word, Randy was a sweet as he always was, but I knew he had a temper because he had shown that to me when we were in college when someone had told him that I was 'going with' one of the professors because they saw me driving his car. He did not ask me anything about the rumor, he just assumed it to be true and told me that he did not like what he had heard and felt that I had betrayed him and instead of hugging and kissing me, he held my shoulders rather tightly and told me that he was not happy with me and he was not going to continue the relationship because I was not the lady he thought I was and tomorrow he would feel the same way and left me standing at the dormitory door.

I was upset and did some irrational things like slamming doors, throwing clothes hangers, cussing and eventually crying. I incurred a headache and took a couple of aspirins and went to sleep. My roommate thought I had taken more aspirins than I did because she claimed that she could not wake me and consequently reported it to the dean of women who was a jerk. She told my roommate and another friend to give me some coffee. When I did wake up, I was angry with them for disturbing my rest. It did little good, because by midnight, the story was out that I tried to commit suicide because Randy had quit me about my relationship with one of the professors! I tried to hold my head up and go on about my business, but I did miss Randy. I soon learned that he missed me too.

At breakfast the next morning, one of Randy's roommates told me that Randy had gone into the shower after having some alcohol and they thought he was trying to drown. He was so upset about his relationship with me. It was hard to believe because he had been so staunch in our parting. The fellow asked me if I would talk to him. I told him that as bad as I felt, I would talk to him if he had come to his senses, but he had told me that it was over and I was trying to get myself together so I could move on.

Randy talked to my roommate and told her that he was wrong in believing what someone else had told him and not asking me anything about the rumor. That same young lady who told him about me driving the car, and I had had an argument the year before when she asked me if Randy knew that I was 'going with' the professor. I spent my wrath upon her with a vengeance from hell. I challenged her to the kind of 'knockdown, drag 'em out fight' like I had witnessed many days in Scroggy because I felt that her mouth had written a check that her hind part could not cash. She balked on the fight, but her mouth stayed in gear to get her something that she did not want.

It now occurred to me that Randy was not just now hearing this rumor. It was something which grew out of riding with the professor to a football game the year before Randy had come to college. A couple of my friends and I had ridden with the professor to the football game because the bus was full. After the game, he took us to a restaurant and ordered food which I did not want and did not eat. That angered him and he told one of his classes about it the next day at school. He wanted to have a relationship with me because my best friend was dating his roommate who was a professor and he had the idea that I was the same kind of girl. Foiled, so he and I only had arguments the rest of the year, even involving me using profanity with him and deciding that I was going to find another college to attend for the next year.

In preparation to attend another college, I went to summer school in Scroggy to enroll as a full fledge sophomore and I was foiled when my mother decided that if I would be further ahead at my present college, then I should return and hurry out to graduate. I was so uptight about it and hoping to figure a way to avoid fresh professors until I was not as sociable as I had been before and more serious minded with a single purpose of mind to get what I really needed to graduate and get away.

Ironically, the first person I encountered on the campus while sitting reading that next year was the professor whom I could not stand. He came anyway and sat on the bench with me and said that he apologized for the way he had treated me; that he had learned that I was a nice girl and not like my best friend. He said that he wanted to adopt me. I told him that I had parents; no need to be adopted. He said that he wished he had a nice daughter like me. He promised to do all he could to promote my college career. He was one of my majoring professors and I was taking all the classes he taught during summer school in Scroggy. I was doing this because he had refused to allow me to enter a class one morning because I did not speak to him as I was going to breakfast and met him on my way. This year, however was different. He was treating me decently, but criticized my choice of a boyfriend and referred to him as a gigolo. That did not change the way I felt. He sponsored the debate team and I was a debater. We traveled to other colleges to debate in Texas and Louisiana. We used the college station wagon and the professor's car to travel. There were six of us who traveled to debate. We were all honor students. Randy never showed me that he disliked my debate status, and I am certain that traveling to debate also fueled the relationship rumor. He came around and apologized to me for his reactions. I accepted his apology and we were in love again. I asked him to find out what is going on before accusing me of anything. He promised that he would. Knowing this side of Randy, I was not surprised as he never stayed angry with me for a long time. In a day or two, he was the sweet person I knew him to be.

True to his word, Randy and I had very few cross words ever again. When we had a difference of opinion, one of us usually stopped talking and that would be the end of the conversation. We usually made decisions together about anything major and anything we did on our own was generally a pleasant surprise for the other. We did many 'do it yourself' projects around our home and worked as a team to get the projects done. We enjoyed working together. After working on a project, sometimes we relaxed afterwards by playing a few games of Tic-Tac-Toe, one of Randy's favorite games or Tonk, one of my favorite card games. A couple of our projects were a storage house, a deck and a closet in the garage. They were fun to do and we felt a degree of fulfillment afterwards.

FAMILY RELATIONSHIPS

Randy's children moved back to Boz one year and did not contact him to let him know that they were back in town. A friend of his saw them at the Bingo Hall and told him about it. He inquired from ex-in-laws until he found that they had established residency in the city and secured their address and went to visit. I went along with him to meet his children. We discovered that his daughter was expecting a child soon and that was one of the reasons that they had moved back to Boz. His daughter and youngest son came to visit with us and spend a night here and there. His oldest son would not visit at all. He would talk to Randy when we visited them, however, and that is when he made Randy aware that he felt that his father did not love him because when he was sick and had to have surgery, he did not come to see him. Randy had to tell him that he had not been aware of his medical problems because he had never been told. He also told him that the only way he knew where they were most of the time is when he would not send the child support payments and then he would be told where they were, until they moved again. Randy assured his son that he had always and would always love him. After that conversation, his second son would visit and play cards or board games with us, but he would not spend any nights with us. Randy accepted them the way he found them.

Before the school year ended, Randy's youngest son who was still in high school came to live with us while his mother and her spouse went back to California to look for a residence in order to move back there. They returned the day of the graduation without notice and ripped their son away from our home dripping with bath water. We did not complain and that night at the graduation ceremony, I noticed that the children's mother was wearing the suit which I had bought for Randy's daughter at Easter time. I did not complain. We learned as I took a picture of the graduate, that they had a rental truck and was on their way out of town this night. Randy did not have much time to talk to his son, so we went to their home to talk with his children after the graduation ceremony and sure enough, they were completing the loading of the U-Haul truck, heading to California. Randy was sorry to see them go as this period of time in Boz had been one of the few times he had been able to see and be around his children since they were very small. He had met his first grandchild, a little girl and I had crocheted a dress for her. She was cute and we had a grandchild who would be about six years old before we saw her again.

In the meantime, Mildred had gotten married again and had a daughter of her own and summertime was our time with her as Mildred had moved to Arlington, Texas and took her baby with her. Mildred had enrolled in graduate school to be a licensed social worker and my mother had gone to live with her to babysit and help her keep her house straight. She and her husband were both away all day so someone had to keep the baby. When the baby was old enough for daycare attendance, Mildred graduated and got a job in Fort Worth and her baby was able to attend a private pre-school. During the summer, she spent that time with me and Randy. The baby, Amber, loved Randy and he loved her. He was able to shower all of his energy and love on her that he had not had the chance to shower on his own children. He was Amber's favorite person, something that we had known a long time.

Mildred was progressing nicely on her job and was so happy until she was expecting another child. Since she was working in Fort Worth, she decided to purchase a home in Fort Worth and shortly afterwards gave birth to a baby boy. The weather was so bad until the baby was a few weeks old before Randy and I could drive to Fort Worth to welcome the new born. The boy was named Jules after his father. He favored David, his maternal grandfather, as a newborn, but as he grew older he looked more like his father.

Jules' father did not want his children to love me and Randy as much as they loved him and his family. He could not get Amber to feel that way because he was in Chicago when she was born and Randy was the first 'father' she knew. But he did tell Jules that Randy was not his grandfather; he was just "plain ole Randy." Amber always called Randy 'Grandpa' and I suppose the only way she really knew his name was when she heard someone else call him and he answered. During the summer when they lived with us, it would be about two weeks before Jules would call Randy 'Grandpa.' Randy loved Jules just as much as he did Amber and I believe he knew this. Both children loved to celebrate the 4th of July with us and we always had a ground top swimming pool for them every summer. Jules had an inner tube because he was not as confident in the water as Amber was. He eventually learned to swim though.

Both children learned to ride a bicycle which we bought them. We had bought Amber tricycles and bicycles and saved them for Jules until he asked me one day if I had bought the tricycle for him. When I told him that it was bought for Amber, he told me, "You haven't bought anything for me." It did not take me long to buy him a bicycle and a Ho gauge train set, since Mildred would not give him the train set which her father had given her after he burned out the engine. I had given the train to David as a birthday present because he had told me that he had never had a train as a child and always wanted one. He stayed up all night and played with it when I gave it to him. When we divorced, he had burned the engine out and he gave it to Mildred. I bought a new engine for her and a Styrofoam platform to put it on, but she refused to give it up for her son. So, Grandma bought him his very own train, but his father was jealous and it ended up in the attic.

Mildred's husband's jealousy and selfishness eventually cause them to get a divorce before the children completed grade school. He did not like her family and only wanted the children to associate with his family. He was mean and cruel to Mildred causing me to eventually have him arrested for hitting me and subsequently whenever Randy and I went to Fort Worth to see Mildred and the children, we stayed at a motel and they visited us there. We did not go to Mildred's house. Amber was in high school when they were divorced and it was only then that we visited Mildred again in her home. Jules, Sr. had moved away from the home. The one exception was when my mother wanted us all to have breakfast together at Mildred's house a couple of weeks before she died. We had been to Wichita Falls to a Masonic meeting and stopped in Fort Worth for a night to see Mildred. The children stayed in the hotel with us that night, but my mother wanted us all to have breakfast together at Mildred's, so we did. We also spent a few minutes at Amber's soccer game before continuing on to Boz. We knew that my mother was weak because she had to have a breathing treatment ever so often but she was much better than she had been when we brought her with us at Christmas time. We took it slow and were always with her to be certain that she was alright. She had been feeling well enough to sew. She had borrowed Mildred's sewing machine in the hotel and made something for her while we were there.

Two weeks later we were shocked with the passing of my mother whom had seemed to be progressing very well. That fateful Thursday morning she left us and it marked the saddest day of my life. I had to arrange for a funeral and the transportation of the body to Scroggy. It was at this time that I also developed a hatred for telephone 'call waiting.' I could not get any rest for the telephone calls from friends and family. I appreciated the calls, but most were long distance and friends at the house refused to tell anyone that I was trying to rest. They would say, "Janet, this is long distance; take this call." When I got to Scroggy and had the telephone connected, it did not have 'call waiting' and I got some rest.

The funeral home in Boz who took care of the body also took it to Scroggy and conducted the funeral and burial there. My aunt in Scroggy took care of the particulars on that end. I stayed on a week to take care of my mother's business which was going to necessitate my eventual move to Scroggy. Randy did not object as my mother had accumulated three houses other than the one she was living in and had the lot where our family home had burned to also care for. The problem was that she had mortgaged the house she was living in and the one she had just paid for to make improvements, a second story on her residence to the tune of $20,000. She had left an insurance policy to Mildred for $10,000 which had a penalty because she had done what I often heard that women did, put her age back when she bought the policy. She had a real age and an insurance age. I could not believe it! With the money in the bank which was in my name and Mildred's insurance money, I was able to pay off the loan which had a penalty if she died before it was paid. No attention was called to it when I inquired. I went back to Boz and finished the school year before I returned to Scroggy to pay off the loan. I had asked Randy how he would feel about living in Scroggy and he said that it would be alright with him so I made applications for employment while taking care of business.

Randy had turned 62 years of age and had suffered some medical problems which caused him to feel that it was time to retire and draw Social Security and that is exactly what he did. He was going to the hospital for surgery the day my mother died and he postponed it until after the funeral. By the end of the school year, he was feeling first rate and ready to take on whatever. As soon as the school year was over, Randy and I packed a few things and headed to Scroggy. We stayed for two months and after no job seemed to be coming through, we prepared to return to Boz when I received a telephone call to come to Vicksburg to meet the school district superintendent. I went as requested, met the superintendent and was sent to the personnel office to complete the paper work for my new job. Randy and I went back to Boz to get a few more items in order for me to prepare for work and to summon the contractors to complete the work on the second floor of the house so we could move into it.

When we returned to Boz, I resigned my teaching position and discovered that I had worked ten years and was eligible for a pension rather than taking a lump one-time payment. I filled out the retirement paperwork and packed all that we could get into three vehicles to take to Scroggy. One of Randy's nieces. Connie, whom had lived with us when she returned to Boz had just gotten a job with the school system and her own apartment and car and was willing to help us to drive to Scroggy and help me get situated at school.

Randy had a suburban; we had a Buick Roadmaster and I had a Cadillac which Connie had driven until she got her own car, and we loaded them up with what we needed until the upstairs was finished and we could move to Scroggy. By October, we were ready to move. I took a leave from my job and we went to Boz, hired a mover and with the help of American Legion and Masonic friends and church and club members we packed up to move to Scroggy. It took all day and at the end of the day, the movers had not taken our clothes out of the closets. We had to go and rent a 19 foot truck to put our clothes in. Fortunately, we had driven only one vehicle to Boz because Randy had to drive the truck and I drove the suburban back to Scroggy. We made it to Scroggy successfully just before the movers arrived. It took all day and part of the night to get the furniture into the house and some of it up to the second floor. That meant that it was the next day before we could empty the rental truck of the clothes. What a mess! It was Christmas before we had the house in order to have company and so we had a party of relatives and old friends. Randy and I had united with the AME church, St. Peter, the one in which I grew up in and we had made a few friends there. Life was good; just missing my mother. I could feel her presence, but knew she was not there. The days that followed I often found myself crying while traveling the thirty plus miles to and from work each day. My mother had not lived to be with us in her house; one which she had planned to be the family home. It had five bedrooms, a living room, dining room, kitchen and an office. There was a three room apartment in the rear which she had planned to dismantle but I decided that we would extend the bedroom and make a den of it and use the kitchen as a laundry room and the living room became a multi-purpose room which Randy referred to as 'the hole.' He spent a lot of time in this room rolling coins which he saved, watching television and sipping the drinks he had in the refrigerator in that room. I used this room to sew and iron and sometimes watched television with Randy. Randy also had my XP computer in this room as I had purchased a Vista for my personal use.

      Once we sold the house in Boz, Randy opened his office machine repair shop. His old boss in Boz gave him some used machines and he purchased some from him. He also ordered some new machines. While I was away teaching school, Randy was learning how to repair VCRs, so this was the new machine which he added to his repair line and he had some new ones for sale. I did his book keeping when I got in from work about three days a week. He kept pretty busy, but his best customers were the banks in Scroggy which often needed machine repairs. The schools had some work for him but were slow to pay. They had an awful kind of requisition method. He repaired adding machines, typewriters, copiers, dictating machines and VCRs. Having his own business was tantamount to Randy. Had we stayed in Boz, he had planned to open a shop there and his former boss was helping him to scout out a place to open. In addition to running his own business, Randy was faithful about closing shop for lunch at which time he either cooked dinner or started it. At any rate, each evening when I got home, dinner was ready. Some days, he would close early and meet me in Vicksburg for dinner, especially if we did not have plans for the weekend.

After about a year at our new home, we had work done in the way of converting the car shed which had a clay floor to a concrete floor and added a steel door. This was encouraged when we went to New Orleans to a family reunion to get back home and find that the Cadillac had been vandalized in the car shed. The antenna was gone and we were told that this was the work of a crack head; that they used the telescoping antenna to smoke crack. Soon, we were putting the vehicles without a burglar alarm in the locked garage. We later built a carport for the 3rd vehicle which had an alarm and we could see it from the window.

Things went along pretty well until my aunt's husband died that March in Chicago. My other aunt and I went to be with her there, and to help her plan his funeral. They did not have any children, so we convinced her to move to Scroggy with me and Randy. She agreed to do so and her sister stayed with her until the school year was over when I could help her to pack to move.

When the school session ended, Randy and I flew to Chicago to help my aunt pack. Other relatives and friends also helped her and when everything was loaded, we cleaned the apartment, took the telephones to 'Ma Bell' and we all spent the night with a close friend. The next day, we rented a van to drive to Scroggy. That was the way my aunt wanted to travel.

We had left our vehicle at the airport, so we abandoned the van at the rental station and drove our vehicle to Scroggy. The moving van arrived on Sunday and deposited my aunt's bedroom suit, her living room furniture and her refrigerator, along with all of her other personal property. It did not take long to get her settled in as we had already made room for everything. She gave her dining room furniture, the other bedroom furniture and her kitchen appliances to my aunt. The mover unloaded those items at her house.

As things settled down, my aunt advised that she wanted someone to care for her on a daily basis as Randy and I were working. We interviewed a few ladies and she chose one who would work five days a week and she paid them minimum wage plus a couple more dollars. This person that she hired fixed her lunch each day as I fixed breakfast before I went to work and Randy cooked dinner. So, they mostly bathed her, took care of cleaning her suite and her personal chores like administering medicines, taking her to the doctor, reading to and with her and basically just being there with her during the day. She had a fairly decent income, so this was not in any way a strain for her. She was always a generous person. She was also generous with me and had always been that way even back in the day when I lived with her. I slept on a Murphy bed and each morning, it seemed that I had feathers in my hair. I had declared then, that I was going to write a book and I would call it, <u>Feathers In My Hair.</u> My aunt laughed and often reminded me of my intentions.

My aunt had her caretaker, Randy was working in his shop feeling happy, though not really turning a profit, but he was happy just to have his own place of business and I was working every day. The first year in business, Randy received an award for new businesses from the business owners club at their annual awards dinner/dance.

The one thing that Randy had failed to do was to get fire insurance. He had paid big bucks for burglar bars and other types of alarms but overlooked fire as the owner of the building in which his business was housed, lived upstairs over the business. That was a major oversight as early one morning we were awakened to alert us that the business was ablaze. Once we got up and got to the store, the heat was so intense that we could not stand on the same side of the street to watch it. The entire building was engulfed. We learned that the owner was in the process of moving to the capital, Jackson and fortunately, he and his family were not there, but the rugs which he sold and kept in the basement of Randy's business were all destroyed. Fortunately for us, we had built a storage house and were no longer keeping our riding lawn mower at the store, but the grandchildren's bicycles were still there. Randy was heartbroken and simply devastated. I went to work that day as school had just opened for the year, but I did not stay. I left early and the fire was still raging. Other nearby fire units had been summoned to help extinguish the blaze. The other tenant in the building did not show up until late in the day and that was unusual. Their business was failing and it seemed that the blaze started in the basement of their store which also contained rugs which the owner sold. Randy and I had bought some which were still stored in the store. We lost everything and had no fire insurance. Randy had built the sales counter and the display tables all by himself and was proud of them. We had purchased a display item from one of my co-workers who had closed her school supply business and a table from the owner of the building. He had closed his rug business when he rented the store to Randy.

Once the blaze was out, there was nothing left in the building. The owner and his wife met with me and Randy and said that he had written a book and all of them burned in his apartment. He was a professor at the local college in the business department. He stated that all of his belongings which he had not moved were also destroyed. The other store owner did not have anything to say and once the fire chief made his report, he stated that the fire started in the basement of the furniture store and declared it to be arson.

Randy was already heartbroken with the loss of his repair tools which he had used at the beginning of his career as an office machine technician. The other stuff lost did not hurt him as much even though he had used his own blood, sweat and tears to put things together. It took a while for him to recover. I did everything that I could to console him. Sometimes he was acceptable of my overtures and sometimes he was not. He and my cousin had often gone to the casinos for recreation and I only went for lunch or dinner, but I began to play the slots with him also, to be with him when he was trying to relax.

We were staunch church goers but we made our way to a casino for dinner on Sunday evening and a little time on the slots. When we went out at night, my other aunt usually came over and spent the night with the one who lived with us. They had a nourishing relationship. They had been bed mates as children and they felt comfortable now. I was happy for them.

After a couple of years with us and proper medical care, my aunt decided to have a hernia which she had been complaining about for years, repaired. She had first decided not to do it, but she claimed that the pain was becoming excessive. She saw the doctor and when he recommended surgery, she told me that she was not going to have it. Then, she changed her mind and decided to do it. I reluctantly went along with her, but felt very uncomfortable about it. Sure enough, when she went to the hospital, the doctor said that he would have to build her up physically before he could do the surgery. That took a week and I felt like telling her to cancel it and my gut said to do it but I went on along with it and the scheduled day of the surgery, I called the hospital to cancel it and they had already done it.

My other aunt and I went to the hospital to be there when she left recovery and we were finally told that she had not regained consciousness and was being transferred to the intensive care unit. They finally let us see her and she was on a ventilator. We were told that the operation was a success, but she was not responding as expected. She did have a pacemaker but it seemed that somehow the anesthesia was not right. She talked to us about going home. We told her that we would take her home and take care of her when she was released from the hospital. She told us that she was going home with Mama and Julia. This was not good, as they were both dead. We visited at each interval that we were allowed to see her and went home for the night to return the next day which was a Sunday. They made us wait and wait before they would let us see her; they said that the doctors were with her and as soon as they were through, that we could see her. When we last saw her they had put her in restraints saying that she was trying to pull her tubes out and saying she had a stroke. We did not believe that and after a while, they came out and told us that she had passed away. They had to close the door because we were disturbing the ICU.

When we finally calmed down, we called a funeral home to pick up the body and made funeral arrangements for Scroggy and Chicago. It was July, so there were no rushes. Randy and I and my other aunt went to Chicago and buried her beside her husband of fifty years. We sadly returned to Scroggy to resume our daily lives and send 'Thank You' notes and missives for our dear departed. I also had to dispose of some of her personal items and give memorabilia to friends and relatives who wanted them. That took a while as she had so many friends. She had been in the dumps since her old schoolmate Beah Richards had died and she would not attend the funeral. Beah had returned to Vicksburg to be with her family, just as my aunt had returned to Scroggy to be with her family. Her old schoolmate Birma Woodhouse who lived in New York had been to visit her and several others since she had come back home. She had not been lonely, but we were now lonely with her gone.

On the plane back to Mississippi, our school's secretary had the seat next to mine. She told me that a new principal had been chosen. I had applied for the job, but was in Chicago when the interviews took place, so I had missed out on the job. Oh well, I said, so what, I will just roll with the punches.

That is exactly what I had to do. Roll with the punches as plenty of them were hurled at me by the newly assigned principal. She came to me the first day and told me that she expected me to help her and that the administration wondered why I was not so cooperative. I was puzzled by this statement but went on as if there was some merit to it. Little did I know that this female had designs to help me to lose my job.

I was assigned a teacher's assistant who wanted to be the teacher. She did not want to do anything that I asked her to do and I learned that she was regularly going into the front door to the principal's office and coming out of the back door as she made her report about me. I acted as though I did not know about this and kept up a friendly facade. She even gave me a Christmas present, as I did her as well. As the year rolled on, one of the first things that made me really wise was the fact that I was not scheduled for a teacher evaluation and the principal had said in a faculty meeting that everyone was doing what they were supposed to be doing except Mrs. Myles. I thought she was joking as she had seemed to be friendly with me when she was a teacher herself. I got the real truth when I inquired about my evaluation date. She told me that she had already done it and it was not good, in the secretary's office. I told her "Fine." She said that I would not be able to get a contract with that evaluation. The secretary suggested that I let her do the evaluation over and give me a chance to do a better evaluation than she said that she had. I agreed. She came into my classroom and sat about fifteen minutes and left. I never saw the finished product.

Ordinarily, students were frisked and checked for illegal objects when entering the building and after a day of absence when I returned to work, I was also frisked and asked to turn over my purse for inspection. I refused and was told that it was believed that I had a pistol in my purse. The next thing that happened to me was when I parked my truck in a handicapped parking space, I was asked to move it though my handicap license plate was visible. I was told that those spots were for visitors and a school security person was there to see to it that I moved it after being asked by the local guard to do so. I moved the truck and wanted to know what the big ruckus was about. The principal told the man from the central office that I just was not a cooperative person. I received a memorandum to meet with the assistant superintendent of the school system about thirty minutes before dismissal time. I saw the principal leaving and I had to arrange for care of my students before I left and I went to Radio Shack and bought a tape recorder to tape the meeting. Unfortunately, when I arrived, the meeting was over so I was advised that we would have it another day. I said OK and called a lawyer who accepted my case when I told him about all of the petty occurrences. There was the window shade thing wherein I had to leave them a certain way every day. There was the thing about where I should place the "In God We Trust" motto in the classroom. After a day of being absence, I returned to find that the principal had moved the sign from where I had put it and demanded that it remain where she had it after I put it back where I had it. She sent the secretary to tell me what I had to do. I callously said, "That woman must want me to whip her butt." Next thing I knew, I had threatened the principal! The next day, the two assistant superintendents from the district office came to visit with me and wanted to know why I had called my husband to come up on the day in which I was made to move my truck. I told them that they were allies in a case against me and I needed to know that there was someone there for me. Naturally, they felt that I was getting ready to assault someone or have him to do it. Boy, I thought the students whom I dealt with were 'something else' but these adults were just as bad or worse. This was the first occasion in which I had a student to lie on me and get a witness to the lie. I will never understand that. I had taught in several states, but the Mississippi children were definitely different and so were the teachers and administrators.

    My year did not improve. One lie about me after another and before the end of the year, one student told me that she did not have to do what I said because the principal told her mother that I was being fired anyway. News travels. I finally got tired of my teaching assistant and when she paid my students to pass the spelling test, I asked to have her moved from my classroom. She was moved and the principal and assistant superintendent permitted her to take a computer to another room which was assigned to me. I also learned that she had taken a copy of one spelling lesson and a test from another and told the principal that I was not testing what I was teaching. On top of that, one of my students accused me of hitting him and the librarian had seem him put the mark on himself. She wrote a statement on my behalf, but when the end of the year rolled around, the principal and an officer from downtown sent the secretary to give me a statement that I would not receive a contract for the coming school year with a list of reasons why I was being terminated. I accepted it and contacted my lawyer.

    I checked my inventory and turned in all of my grades and every paper which I needed to get myself checked out at the end of the school year. I prepared for a hearing. I had proof of the inaccuracies, distortions and lies which had been told on me. On the night before the hearing, my lawyer's father who was also a lawyer, called me to state that the hearing would be postponed as his son-in-law had been badly burned in an explosion and they were all at the hospital, but that I would have my hearing.

    The hearing did not take place, but I did have several depositions because I had filed a suit with the EEOC (Equal Employment Opportunity Commission). I had filed this suit when a young man at the school was assigned the job of assistant principal when he did not have a certificate in administration and I did. I also had more experience than he had. That was the beginning of my serious harassment. I did not step back and my lawyer supported me. With the EEOC case file and my rebuttal of the allegations concocted at the school, the school lawyer got my lawyer to agree that instead of me being fired, they would give me a 'no negative' recommendation to teach elsewhere. I accepted the offer, but continued to pursue the discrimination suit after my retirement. The school invited me to the retirement ceremony the next year. I asked in the Rsvp by telephone if they really expected me to show up. They did, so the secretary told me and stated that they had to ask me to come. They sent me the teacher retirement pin and certificate in the mail as I did not show up, which I believe I put in the trash, because I have no idea where they are.

Upon that retirement, Randy and I took a two week cruise in Northern Europe, visiting nine countries. We flew to England where we boarded the ship in Dover and cruised over to France and got a bus to Paris where we spent an entire day sightseeing and having lunch on a boat on the Seine River. We were impressed in St. Petersburg, Russia where a man drew Randy's profile as we walked while in line, to the tomb of Peter the Great. He gave the man $5.00 for the drawing. We rolled it up and brought it home and put it in a frame.

Every country that we visited was really impressive. We returned home on a plane from Stockholm, Sweden. When we returned it was time for a family reunion which I hosted and we celebrated 25 years of family reunions.

Randy and I had already been to Las Vegas earlier in the year and we needed to slow down some, so we spent a weekend at an Indian casino in the northern part of the state to rest away from everyone and everything. We had the 'go spirit' so we went to our church's conventions, the Masonic conventions and the next year, we went on a Caribbean cruise for a week and had a wonderful time, except I contracted a fungus in a Mayan ruin and Randy planted a pecan on the top of a ziggurat. He said that it would become tree, he hoped.

We had been traveling for fun, but Randy was directed to go to a clinic on the Gulf Coast for an examination as he had filed a law suit claim based on asbestos damage. Before that trip, we had gone to Baton Rouge to care for one of my cousins whom had had surgery. She did not have any children and her husband had died. So we spent a week with her and then went on to see about Randy's asbestos tests.

I did not know about Randy's medical history because he had not shared a lot of it with me as I was working every day and he was seeing his doctor while I was working. Those were some of the days he would meet me in Vicksburg and have dinner and play slots at the casino. I learned more after retirement.

Just before we planned to take a cruise to Hawaii, Randy's doctor ordered oxygen for him to use. He had been having breathing tests and treatments which I knew nothing of and then finally he had to have a nebulizer. I checked the internet to see if the oxygen would be allowed on the airplane and found no restrictions. It was when we were ready to board the plane that Randy's oxygen was confiscated. One of the checkers told him that she would keep it in her locker until he returned from his trip. We took the long flight to Dallas, Texas and from there to Hawaii. That was not so bad, but coming back was a problem as we were assigned to one of American Airline's smallest planes out in the middle of nowhere from which we had to have a bus to get to. The walking distance as well, got to Randy and I had to get a wheelchair for him. He told me to take Mildred with me on my next trip because he was not going. Once back home, Randy used his oxygen regularly but not continuously. He would use it when he felt that he needed it. He always had it with him when he left home, but he would leave it in the car and go to it when he felt like it. He was also given a concentrator for use at home when he slept. He used it every night. Later, he was introduced to liquid oxygen which was easier to handle and had a tank with which he could fill his personal container when needed. Things were looking up until Randy was diagnosed with type 2 diabetes. Now, he had to monitor his glucose and his intake of sugar. He took it in stride and continued to enjoy life, though he did slowdown in his physical activities. He told me to get someone to cut the grass. I had to hire someone to cut the front yard inside and outside the fence. I rode the tractor and did the lots behind our house. Randy's body had gotten weaker but he kept a strong will. He could not help me as much as he had in the past, but he still did what he could do without too much trouble. He enjoyed helping me so I never discouraged him.

Randy also delighted in my Mildred's daughter who was in college and living with us. He was always on her side, no matter what she did, good or bad. That was his baby and he was her 'Paw Paw." She always said that his grandchildren just did not know what they were missing. He even went one hundred miles with her to go to court on a traffic ticket with his oxygen in tow. When she graduated from college, he could barely walk but he was there with his oxygen.

In the meantime, we started going to the veteran's hospital as Randy was a veteran. They found us eligible for treatments, but eventually there was a copay due which was not billed until after Randy died. Settlement of that bill held up the finalizing of his will.

After four years of depending upon oxygen, Randy was hospitalized at the Veteran's hospital and a senseless intern told him in the ward where he was lying, in the earshot of the other patients and anyone else in the room, that he had approximately two months to live as he now needed at least eleven liters of oxygen constantly. When I learned this, I hit the ceiling and discussed it with the social worker and threatened to sue. I was as mad as swindled robber! I made arrangements to take Randy home, but learned that he had to be taken home in an ambulance because the adequate amount of oxygen needed for transportation was not available to me or the supplier.

So, I had to leave Randy in the hospital until his oxygen supplier could get to our house and hook up two concentrators to deliver eleven liters of oxygen at the same time. That took a while, and in the meantime, our medical supplier was searching for oxygen tanks the size of the ones in the ambulance, so Randy could be transported to Fort Worth to our new home. Sadly, on the day that the supplier called me and told me that he had found two tanks and they would each be equipped with a valve so I would not have to try to change one to the other as Mildred's co-worker who was an ambulance driver, had suggested. He had advised that we stop at a fire station and have them change the valve for us. At the same time, Mildred's co-worker had told her that if we could not get the adequate oxygen tanks, he would come to Scroggy and pick Randy up. Randy fought hard with a strong will, but gave up the ghost two days after the Medicare program in Texas which I had enrolled him, became effective.

    This was a most sad time; in the middle of packing to move, trying to sell our house, trying to keep Randy comfortable and now having to prepare for the transportation of Randy's body to Texas and the funeral. I was overwhelmed, but friends came to the rescue. My friend Pearl had been with me and spent some nights so I could get some sleep while Randy was almost helpless. My neighbor, Mary and her daughters, Verna and Nadine and Eva from church, put in some hours helping me to finish packing. They were a Godsend and constantly in my prayers.

    The move date had to change from March to April as Randy died at the beginning of March. My first visit to our new home was when I went to the funeral in Boz and stopped to see the house we had purchased as Mildred had taken care of all of the transactions. I took the large potted plant which had been given to me by the Preservation Commission on which I had been a member, to our new house. I left the plant there while I went to the funeral and back to Scroggy to finish packing and move. That took the next three weeks to complete. The movers finished loading after two days and headed to Texas with my belongings. I left the next day after spending the night with Pearl. I was alone and drove the long weary trip by myself which usually always was with Randy. Missing him was almost unbearable. All along the highway, there were memories that we had made together. Again, I was driving and shedding tears. I was wondering how I was going to survive in the big city of Fort Worth, Texas, ALONE.

NEW HOME ALONE

I arrived in Fort Worth and spent the night with Mildred. I rose early the next morning and purchased some items to clean the kitchen and bathrooms and went onward to the house. The movers arrived that same evening and spent the night in a motel. Mildred gave them directions to the new home. She opened the house so they could get inside. I got there later as I had to get some breakfast before my day started. Five men moved my belongings into the house and they were not finished until nine o'clock that night. They were ready to go and so was I.

Thanks that the beds were put together. Mildred helped me to put linen on one of the beds and wash some things that had been soiled. That was a mess as the faucet leaked so badly that I had to call a plumber right away. This was my greeting to my new home. It was new to me, but actually about thirty years old. It had been a good deal for me, as I was able to pay for it while trying to sell the house from which I had moved. There were many things which needed repairs as I discovered as the days went by. Fortunately, Mildred had purchased some home appliance insurance for which I had to only pay $60.00 per repair visit. That was some relief.

It was a long time before I had most of the essential items unpacked. I had a path throughout the house until Christmas. I did all of the unpacking by myself. Mildred and her daughter were both working and her son was away in college, so I had no help. Furthermore, Mildred stated that unpacking would be good therapy for me during my time of grief. I was left with no choice except to do the best that I could alone.

There were other things to get done; finding my way around a new neighborhood, meeting my neighbors and learning about the neighborhood's do's and don'ts. I also needed a church home and I needed to find some friends. Nights were lonely; Randy and I had been married for thirty years and now I was alone. I cried myself to sleep some nights until I discovered where the cassette tapes were that we used to send to each other before we were married. I played them a few nights and to hear his voice helped me quite a bit. I was able to sleep better.

    I wanted to have a garden, but I had to have a forty year old American elm tree cut down before my backyard would see some sunlight. This tree had also damaged the roof on the house. It was not until a fierce thunderstorm occurred that I learned that the roof repair was not adequate. I called the roofers back so much until I just decided to pray to God for a repair as the quote which I had received was just out of sight.

    I worked at getting my college's local alumni chapter revived and found one schoolmate with whom I talked and socialized. I had found a friend and made a few acquaintances during the revival. Mildred got me to enroll in the fitness club where she had a membership and she paid for my first two years. I was basically involved in the water aerobics, but sometimes I would do the treadmills and bicycles and the stretch class. Zumba was too much for me, so one try at that was enough. I did however; make a couple of friends in the water aerobics classes

and therefore increased my friendship list. It was later that I was asked to join a bowling league. I gained three more friends and a number of acquaintances from bowling. Soon, I was able to entice my friends to play Bridge. They already played Keno once a month and invited me to go along. There, I met more friends and acquaintances. Life was beginning to take on more meaningfulness. I had an array of activities. The only thing missing was a male companion.

CYBER GAMES

About two months before the anniversary of Randy's death, Mildred and my granddaughter felt that perhaps I should try to meet a male companion. They suggested that I sign on to one of the dating sites. I wanted a male companion, but I really did not want one, because every time I looked at a man or one said something to me, all I could see was Randy. If I could not see Randy in a man, I did not want to spend any time with him. I finally decided to give it a try.

Dating sites come with a price. I decided to sign up for a three month trial. During this time, I actually met a man who was the same age as I and we had lunch one Saturday at a restaurant which was not too far for either of us. He was a very nice gentleman and brought me flowers on this first date. We talked at lunch sharing some things about ourselves. He was a bit shorter than his profile picture and looked a lot like a short David though he was soft spoken like Randy, had a graduate degree and had been a career military man. He had retired from the Government Accounting Office. Aside from being too short for me, he had not dressed the part of a professional man. He wore a flop down hat, black un-pressed jeans and a tee shirt. On the profile picture he had on a dress suit and hat. I was disappointed as I had dressed to impress. I told him that I did not really feel that I was ready for a relationship and thanked him profusely for lunch and his patience with me. He said that it was not a problem. We had each other's telephone numbers but I did not plan to call him in the future. We had each other's e-mail addresses as well. I decided that I would e-mail him. He beat me to the punch! He said that he felt that we should not continue our relationship because he had an enlarged prostate and felt that this was not fair to me. I answered him that I appreciated his kindness, concern for me and thanked him for the beautiful flowers, lunch and his gentle status. I wished him well on his physical condition hoping that it would turn out as he hoped.

While I was on this site, a young airman flirted with me and I told him that he was too young for me. In his profile, he was 39 years old and had been in the Air Force for 19 years. His answer to me was that he was attracted to me regardless of our ages. I told him that I appreciated his interest, but I was not into younger men; I was looking for someone my age or close to it. Before my time on the site ended, he flirted with me again. I brushed him off and was soon not active on the site. I shut it down and dropped the idea of meeting a man on the wide, wide web. That was at the end of January.

Time would move on and by July, I had to rescue my 91 year old aunt from her daughter and grandson, whom had caused her home to be foreclosed. She had encountered a stroke and when they took over her affairs, everything went to pot! Keeping her and taking care of her put a great limitation on my activities. I had to drop water aerobics and find a day care where she could stay while I bowled on Wednesdays. It was not until I found a facility which would keep her the three days I could financially afford that I could resume water aerobics. From July to November, tension was rising and by November, I had cabin fever! I decided to try the dating site for Black people. I signed up for six months. It did not take long that I started receiving flirts and messages from males on the site. I felt that there was a possibility of there being 'the one.'

The first flirter that I responded to told me that he was Robert, a highway patrolman and he also refereed high school basketball games. He declared that he was divorced and the lady of his life was his 90 year old mother. He did not have a picture with his profile but asked for my e-mail address so he could send me a picture. I responded and he sent me a picture of a man dressed in a referee uniform, holding a basketball on a gym floor. He gave me his telephone number and asked me to call him. I did. We talked and that following Sunday, he called me. During this telephone call, we agreed to meet at a restaurant in the nearby small town as he lived in Dallas.

    I got ready for our meeting and got on the highway to meet this man. He called me just as I was entering the city limits of the nearby town to tell me that he would not be able to meet me because there was a job assigned to him that had to be completed. I said OK and turned around and went back home. I was disappointed but took it like a soldier. He called me later and apologized and set up another meeting. This time, the meeting would be in a town closer to Dallas. I drove to the destination and sat and waited and waited and called him, to get no answer. I decided to use common sense and went home. When I arrived at my house, there was a message on my answering machine from him that he would not be able to meet me but would reimburse me for my gas used in the trip. I was hopping mad! Why is this happening to me? He called me that night with a lame excuse. I told him how I felt about when the dog bites you once, it's his fault and that if he bites you twice, then it's your fault. He told me that he was not a dog. I questioned that and told him that I felt that he really did not want to meet me. He swore that he did want to meet me but he had obligations to his job that had to be fulfilled. I softened a little bit but felt that this was a hopeless case. I told him that had I been younger I would be crying and past upset, but I was taking this like an adult and planned to move on, perhaps without him and said goodnight and goodbye.

    About a week later, this same man called me and told me that he was sick. I told him that I already knew that but I was not a doctor. He swore that he had been to the doctor and was feeling really bad, but wanted to talk to me, maybe I could help him to feel better. I asked him why he called me and his sorry answer was that he needed me. I let him talk and finally told him to take his medicine, go to bed and get some rest.

A few days later, Robert called and told me that he had to put his truck in the shop and was waiting for his brother to pick him up and thought he would call me. He wanted to arrange a meeting for us. I agreed, hoping that this time it would work, or 'three strikes and you are out.'

I was not eager to meet Robert because I had decided that he was full of it. Sure enough, he called me about an hour before we were meeting to tell me that he had to go to a CPR class. I told him that I understood and hoped it was a learning situation. I later sent him an e-mail around Easter, which was the next week, and told him that had Jesus been at his CPR meeting, he would have learned something about resurrection. He sent me some more e-mails about joining a Deal Whale and something else with a virus in it. I sent it back to him and told him not to send me any more viruses. He told me that he was sorry. I told him that I was aware of that, but keep his e-mails. We stopped communicating as I summed him up as a real jerk that probably was still married. He told me that his son and daughter had finished college and that he too had graduated from a college in East Texas, where I suspected that he met his wife and was still with her.

Though Robert and I never met, I had not completely cut myself off from other males on the dating site. There were a number of young men who flirted with me and I talked to a 50 year old whom I told that he, too, was too young for me. He asked me to remember him if I lowered my acceptance age as he really wanted to get to know me, as he liked older women. He always seemed to lean that way, he said. He had a teenaged son who lived with him and that he was divorced. I told him that should I decide younger, I would let him know.

Then, to my surprise, the airman whom I had met on the Match site, flirted with me on this site. He was still talking about how attracted he was to me. I told him that I rather felt that I reminded him of someone whom he was fond of and perhaps that is why he felt that way. He assured me that he was well aware of our age differences, but he just had to give credit where credit was due. I brushed him off again, but this time, he popped up on a regular basis talking smack to me. He had a webcam and suggested that I get one as he would like to see me and talk to me if I did not mind. He said so many nice things until I almost felt obligated to get a webcam, something which had never run across my mind in any way. I really did not know what a webcam was or really how to use it. So, I traipsed off to Wally World and bought a webcam. I was able to install it myself. One could use a webcam on the dating site if you had one. I did not have one, but the airman did have one which he used. After I got the webcam, he showed me how to set up Messenger which I had never even thought of either. E-mail had been all I needed in the cyber world. With Messenger, we could talk off the dating site. It was fun to me. I discovered that many of my e-mail friends were also users of Messenger. Since the airman was only 40 years old now, I felt that I may as well talk to the 50 year old as well.

The 50 year old had a webcam, so we could talk and use it. One of my old friends in Louisiana told me that he had another video site and he introduced me to ooVoo. I got the 50 year old to talk to me on that site as well. On our very first conversation, the name that he gave me was phony. When my daughter asked me what he told me it was, she said, "That's the name of a baseball player on the Ranger team."

The next conversation that we had I told the man about his lie. He apologized profusely and stated that he had to be sure that it was OK to tell me the truth. He then said that his name was "Mike." He gave me a last name, but his e-mail said that he was Glen Black and that is the name he used for Messenger and ooVoo. I accepted his nom de guerres for what they were worth. He was someone to talk to when I wanted to talk to someone. We exchanged pictures, telephone numbers and e-mail addresses but not physical addresses. He told me that he lived in Tyler,

Texas and I told him that I was in Fort Worth. We made tentative plans to meet, but never a place or a date. We talked about many things over a three year period such as his love for baseball and frequent trips to Arlington to see the games. He was also an avid golf player and could teach me to play golf. On and on this went until I had to go to Tyler for some business and asked him to meet me at a cafeteria. He had a meeting to go to and could not meet me. Fine. That was my signal. I did not talk to him anymore. When he tried to contact me on Messenger, I ignored him, basically because I was talking to someone else and refused to give him any more of my time. He only tried one more time to contact me. I am sure he knew that we were over.

Before I severed contact with "Mike" I was seduced by a fast acting, fast talking young man who sent me two pictures of himself, he said, and told me if I like them, to let him know because he thought I was gorgeous. You can imagine that I just basked in his praise! He lifted me and my spirit though he was younger than the airman according to him but he was so intelligent! He swept me off my feet and before I knew it, I was in love. I had never had such a learned conversation with a man! We exchanged telephone numbers and some mornings when I got up, I would have a text message from him telling me how he dreamed of me etc.; stuff I loved to hear and read. Then sometimes he would call me while I was bowling and put a smile on my face. He told me that he had graduated from Morehouse and that he was an off-shore scientist for an oil company, and that he was at that time on a rig getting some training that was required once a year. When his training was over, he planned to move to Arlington, as he was being re-located from the Atlanta area. He planned to buy a house and looked forward to entertaining me when he was situated. That sounded magnificent to me. I did not have to hear what any other man said. This sexy man had swept me off my feet like none other before. He was intelligent, educated, had a sexy voice and knew all of the right things to say to me to make me want him. He told me that his name was Omar.

I was planning to attend a family reunion in Mississippi and told him about it. He told me that he was from Mississippi and his telephone had a Mississippi area code. He asked me which hotel I would stay in and if he had a chance, he would meet me there. Wow! This was too good to be true. And like the old saying, "If it sounds too good to be true, it usually is." I had read my horoscope a few days before this and it warned me that my love life would come to a sudden halt. I thought nothing of it until it was six months later when I finally heard from him. This was a priceless horoscope coincidence. I healed.

I was surprised to hear from Omar and told him so. He claimed that he had lost his father during the summer and had been transferred to Ontario rather than Arlington and that he just did not care anymore. He apologized for not telling me before. I told him that I had gotten over him after having fallen in love with him. He sent me another picture; supposedly him, while we were talking and I told him that all of his pictures were different; how so? He claimed that all of mine were different. I told him that my pictures had dates on them and his did not. He requested a video chat and I complied to find that I never saw him. The next time he requested a chat with me; I complied but covered my camera and told him the same lie that he told me about a closed circuit in his work place. I did see him this time and he did not favor any of the pictures he had sent to me. Again, he countered with my not looking like my pictures. We argued and about every three to six months, he contacts me to say 'hello.' It is OK. He is just one of my acquaintances now; a 'friend.' This all happened after I saw him on the video while talking to me and I recognized him as a newscaster, relocated from Atlanta to the Dallas area who was indeed married with two adult sons. Instead of being 36 years old, he was 46. He had not attended Morehouse but Howard University. He was originally from New York, not Mississippi. I did not tell him what I knew, but I did tell him that I knew who he was. He has never attempted to deny that I might know who he was.

In the meantime, as I was busy getting Omar out of my mind, I talked more to Mike and the airman, Clinton. I knew that Mike and I were not going anywhere. He was never specific about anything and talking about the weather with him was about as good as anything. On the other hand, it appeared that everything that Clinton told me about himself was true. He told me where he was and what he did every day. He claimed that he was divorced and had one son who was Clinton the 5th, as he was Clinton the 4th. He was a recruiter in the Air Force. After talking to him for almost a year, I checked him out and found his address and Facebook page. When I joined Facebook, I invited him to be a 'friend' but he did not respond. It was not long after that, when he shut his Facebook page down and removed his identifying information from the Internet. He did become a part of LinkedIn, however, and information there verified his Air Force status. I did not tell him that I had checked him out, but what I had learned gave me some idea that he was genuine. Clinton would contact me on Messenger or Skype about once every month. I enjoyed talking with him and when I did not hear from him for several months, he would tell me that he had been overseas and just got back. I did not question him. He always talked about coming to Texas, to San Antonio where all airmen get their basic training. He would tell me that he was coming at a certain time and for two years; he was going to see me when he came to Texas.

The first time he came to Texas, he contacted me but said that he had a military vehicle and was not able to drive to Fort Worth. I said OK. The next time he came to Texas, he claimed that he had to hurry back to his post and did not have time to contact me. Then, year three, he told me the date that he would be arriving in San Antonio and he would see me. I asked him for a telephone number where I could contact him when he arrived. He gave me a cellular telephone number and told me that it was charging at the present. I sent him an e-mail and told him that I was going to take a train to San Antonio and wanted to know where he would be staying so I could reserve a hotel nearby. He contacted me by

Messenger and told me that the date had been moved to September. He would not be making an August trip, but he would tell me the date as soon as he had it. I told him OK. In the meantime, I got my telephone whiz kid, my granddaughter to check out the telephone number which he gave me. She said, "Grandma, this is a Text Plus App." I said, "Good. I have been going down a one way street with this man and it is time for me to make a right turn!" The next time he contacted me, I let him know what he had done. He was so apologetic but could not deny what he had done. He could never get the words out of why he did it. All he could say was that he did not want to hurt me and how sorry he was that he had hurt me. He did not know why.... I told him that I knew why. He had always known what he was doing; he just never let me know. He had contacted me because he had to get up to go to the bathroom and saw that I was online and decided to talk to me because he was so attracted to me and did not know why. I told him that I should have been showing up 'busy.' He said, "I did", but he knew I was online. I was busy and I told him so. I told him to go back to bed and go to sleep. That was my last contact with Clinton. I decided that there just is not another 'the one' out there for me. I trusted him and I had told him just as I told the others, that I require the truth and respect. Those are the two things which I require of a significant other. It appears that even the most truthful men on the dating sites are 'CATFISH.' That is how I sum up the Cyber Games.

    Currently, I am spending my time keeping my health updated, bowling, playing Bridge and Keno when I can, going to the Casino occasionally, doing water aerobics several times a week and going to church regularly and the symphony with season tickets. As soon as I can see where I can work it in, I plan to take a cruise to the Eastern Caribbean with hopes of no more 'feathers in my hair.'

CPSIA information can be obtained
at www.ICGtesting.com
Printed in the USA
LVHW082204140223
739550LV00031B/849